G000135220

THE RESURRECTION MEN

Adrian Jones.

THE RESURRECTION MEN

WALES'S GRAND SLAM 2008

PAUL REES

MAINSTREAM
PUBLISHING

EDINBURGH AND LONDON

For Margaret

First published in Great Britain in 2008 by
MAINSTREAM PUBLISHING COMPANY (EDINBURGH) LTD
7 Albany Street
Edinburgh EH1 3UG

ISBN 9781845964214

A catalogue record for this book is available
from the British Library

Typeset in Caslon and MetaPlus

Printed in Great Britain by
Clays Ltd, St Ives plc

ACKNOWLEDGEMENTS

A BIG THANK YOU TO THE FOLLOWING FOR THEIR HELP in the preparation of this book: Mike Averis, of *The Guardian*; Dick Best, the former England and Lions coach; Ben Clissitt, the sports editor of *The Guardian* for again agreeing to time off without any notice; Brendan Fanning, the rugby correspondent of the *Sunday Independent* in Dublin and author of a seminal book on Irish rugby in the professional era, *From There to Here*; Danno Heaslip, the president of Galwegians Rugby Club; David Llewellyn, of *The Independent*, for making numerous corrections to the text and offering constant encouragement; Ian McGeechan, the director of rugby at Wasps; Nigel Melville, the chief executive of United States Rugby; Mike Ruddock, the director of rugby at Worcester; Andy Selby, of SAS, the official data supplier for the RBS Six Nations; Corris Thomas, the Head of Game Analysis at the International Rugby Board; Andy Wilson, *The Guardian's* rugby league correspondent; and Bill Campbell and Paul Murphy at Mainstream Publishing.

CONTENTS

WALES'S GRAND SLAM 2008

2 February 2008 – England 19 Wales 26
(Twickenham)

9 February 2008 – Wales 30 Scotland 15
(Millennium Stadium)

23 February 2008 – Wales 47 Italy 8
(Millennium Stadium)

8 March 2008 – Ireland 12 Wales 16
(Croke Park)

15 March 2008 – Wales 29 France 12
(Millennium Stadium)

2008 RBS Six Nations Championship Table

	Team	P	W	D	L	F	A	PTS
1	WALES	5	5	0	0	148	66	10
2	ENGLAND	5	3	0	2	108	83	6
3	FRANCE	5	3	0	2	103	93	6
4	IRELAND	5	2	0	3	93	99	4
5	SCOTLAND	5	1	0	4	69	123	2
6	ITALY	5	1	0	4	74	131	2

1

From Black to All Black

> There's a light around you.
> I've come to switch it on.
>
> *Gordon Lightfoot*

16 **March 2008. Roger Lewis, the chief executive** of the Welsh Rugby Union, is standing in the foyer of the Wales squad's hotel in the Vale of Glamorgan. Weary players run a gauntlet of autograph seekers as they make their way to the car park some 17 hours after clinching the Grand Slam by defeating France at the Millennium Stadium. Lewis's mind wanders back to another Sunday morning, not six months before, when he had turned up at the team hotel in Pornichet, near Nantes in the north-west of France. There were no scenes of joy or souvenir-hunting fans then; instead of leaving for the airport to fly to Marseille to prepare for a World Cup quarter-final against South Africa, the players and management had packed for a lunchtime flight to Cardiff, where they were to arrive under a cloud rather than be greeted by the warmth of the sun. Their tournament, courtesy of a 38–34 defeat to Fiji in Nantes, was over before the knockout stage had started. Lewis had come to tell the squad that the head coach Gareth Jenkins, who had only been appointed 16 months earlier after Wales's failure to build on the 2005 Grand Slam, had been fired. The WRU was on familiar ground as it started the hunt for its 13th coach in 19 years.

Nantes has been twinned with Cardiff since 1964. It was described by *Time* magazine in 2004 as 'the most liveable city in all of Europe', but to Jenkins it marked the last stop on the road to perdition. The WRU board of directors had met hours after the reverse to Fiji and decided on summary dismissal. Other countries who endured unsuccessful World Cup campaigns, such as Ireland and New Zealand, opted for a lengthy review process before determining the fates of their head coaches. Failure to win the World Cup in the past had meant automatic dismissal for All Blacks' coaches, but Graham Henry, the man who had established the base at the Vale of Glamorgan when he was in charge of Wales between 1998 and 2002, was to survive against all the odds. Jenkins had asked to be judged on how Wales performed at the World Cup, and the WRU took him at his word, a contrast to the Rugby Football Union in 1999 when the then England head coach Clive Woodward had said the same thing but survived, despite a media campaign against him, when England were knocked out by South Africa in the quarter-finals. The rest is history.

It is doubtful that Jenkins would have kept his job even if Wales had beaten Fiji. A proud, passionate man, who had long coveted the post, having been, over the years, the most successful domestic coach in Wales at first with Llanelli and then Llanelli Scarlets, he found himself constrained by the problems he had inherited, and having taken so long to clamber to the top of his greasy pole, he was never able to achieve any sort of grip and quickly slithered back down. Instead of building on the 2005 Grand Slam success, Wales had, as they had done on the two other occasions in the previous twenty years when they had tasted success (1988 and 1994), imploded. Jenkins took over with a recriminatory odour in the air following the abrupt departure of Mike Ruddock on the night of St Valentine's Day, 2006. The official reason for Ruddock's leaving one month after the WRU had said that it was ready to sign a new contract with him was that he wanted to spend more time with his family, but it quickly emerged that other factors were involved, even if there was an absence of anyone willing to go on the record.

At the start of 2007, Jenkins gave a presentation to the coaches of Wales's four regional sides entitled: The Welsh Way – Winning 20.10.07. It was a reference to the date of the World Cup final, and he gave a diluted version of his address to the media. 'You have to be realistic, but there is nothing wrong with being ambitious,' he said. 'I want to coach a team that can win the World Cup. It cannot be an empty mission statement. When I spoke to the players last September, only one or two believed it could happen. I believe we have a better chance of winning the World Cup this year than ever before. There is nothing new about the Welsh Way: the game is about scoring tries, and that is what

Welsh players like to do, but to win the Six Nations and the World Cup we have to create the right environment and sometimes play beyond our best.'

Wales came nowhere near their best in the 2007 Six Nations, winning only one match, against England on the final weekend. Two of their four World Cup group matches were in Cardiff, but defeat to Australia meant they had to beat Fiji in their last match to qualify for the quarter-finals. Wales outscored the islanders by five tries to four in what turned out, despite the tight game plan devised by Jenkins and his coaching team, to be a game of sevens – a contest to see who could score the best try. In 80 minutes, it summed up an overriding problem with the side since the 2005 Grand Slam. That success was based on an off-loading, counter-attacking game. When first Ruddock and then Jenkins tried to instil a more pragmatic approach as opponents quickly devised ways of counteracting a style that was as one-dimensional as a ten-man game plan, they met with resistance and players made their disaffection with Jenkins's tactics known publicly during the World Cup.

Little more than a week after paying off Jenkins, who had seven months of his £180,000 a year contract to run, Lewis boarded a flight to New Zealand, along with the WRU chairman David Pickering and the former Wales and Lions wing Gerald Davies, a member of the union's board of directors. Aware that a number of countries would probably have coaching positions to fill in the coming weeks, they were anxious to gain one advantage from Wales's early exit from the World Cup. Even before they left, the trio were linked with a number of names from the southern hemisphere: Jake White, who little more than a week later would win the World Cup with

South Africa; John Mitchell, New Zealand's coach in the 2003 World Cup who had assisted Ireland and England in the 1990s; Steve Hansen, the New Zealand assistant coach who had been in charge of Wales between 2002 and 2004 before returning home to rejoin Henry; Robbie Deans, Mitchell's assistant between 1999 and 2003 who was coaching Canterbury Crusaders; and Warren Gatland, the former Ireland coach who had enjoyed four highly successful seasons at Wasps before returning to Waikato.

Lewis had canvassed the views of players after the Fiji defeat, and the WRU determined that leadership would be the single most important quality of the new head coach. 'We need somebody who is tough,' said Pickering before the New Zealand trip. 'We are looking for somebody who demands high standards and who has experience of coaching at the highest level. They have to be able to manage professional and demanding athletes and have a clear direction in which they want to take the team.' The words leadership, direction and toughness were to recur frequently during the 2008 Six Nations campaign; Ruddock's attempts to empower players had rebounded on him, while Jenkins, unable to mould a squad in his own image after taking over so close to a World Cup, never managed to exert his authority in the way he had at Llanelli. 'We came in with a very mature attitude towards the players,' said Nigel Davies, Jenkins's backs coach who by the end of 2007 had become the WRU's head of rugby development. 'They were internationals, and we felt they could manage themselves. We looked to involve them in the decision-making process, but, on reflection, while Welsh players want latitude on the field, they demand direction off it. They crave certainty.'

Lewis, Pickering and Davies spent four days in New

Zealand, but their work was effectively done before they had left Auckland Airport. They met Gatland there after he had made the 90-minute drive from his home in Hamilton. Ironically, given the Ruddock affair, he had been released as Ireland's head coach in 2001 amid allegations that some senior players had opposed the renewal of his contract. He played 17 times for the All Blacks at hooker without winning a cap and was a member of the 1989 tour party to Wales and Ireland. Ireland had spent most of the 1990s involved in a tussle with Wales to avoid the wooden spoon, and Gatland, who had ended his playing career at Galwegians before coaching Connacht, slowly led them out of the wilderness, blooding players who were to become household names such as Brian O'Driscoll and Ronan O'Gara. It was at Wasps where Gatland forged his reputation: his successes included the Heineken Cup in 2004, and the left-hand corner on the south side at Twickenham where the scrum-half Robert Howley scored the decisive try in the final against Toulouse was to be the scene of a decisive moment in Wales's 2008 Grand Slam campaign.

The interview with Gatland was followed by one with Deans in Christchurch and another with Andrew Hore, the former Wales conditioning coach, in Wellington. Hore was being lined up for a new position being created in the union, the head of elite rugby; in the event, he turned it down and accepted a similar job with the Ospreys. The trio held two meetings with Henry, not to sound him out about a return to Wales, but to pick his mind. Pickering had been Henry's first team manager when the New Zealander arrived in Wales in 1998, and Henry had never lost interest in the country he had called home for nearly four years. Deans had told the WRU delegation, politely, that he was not interested in coaching Wales. New Zealand had just been dumped out of the World Cup by the hosts France in Cardiff at the quarter-final stage, and Henry was tipped for the sack after New Zealand's worst ever World Cup campaign. It looked a no-brainer, especially after the New Zealand Rugby Union admitted it would be looking for a new coach. Deans, never mind his involvement in the previous abortive World Cup campaign, was widely regarded as Henry's successor, and he was clearly waiting for the call. He ended up being invited to put his name forward for the post only to lose out to Henry, who at the last moment had decided to reapply. Deans was then headhunted by Australia and became the first non-national to take charge of the Wallabies.

Lewis reflected later that it had taken him less than two minutes after meeting Gatland to realise that his search had ended almost as soon as it had started. It might have been different had Stirling Mortlock, the Australia captain, not missed a last-minute penalty in the World Cup quarter-final against England at the Stade Vélodrome in Marseille. Reports in New Zealand had suggested that the RFU was interested in persuading Gatland to return to England, and a salary of £350,000 a year was mentioned. Had Mortlock's kick gone over, England would have been on their way home with their head coach Brian Ashton almost certainly facing the sack, but the wind dragged the ball wide at the last moment, and the holders went on to reach the World Cup final after defeating France in the last four. Ashton held on to his post after surviving a two-month review, but by then Gatland was two weeks into his job with Wales.

'I was not aware of any interest from England,' said Lewis. 'One of the reasons we moved so quickly was that we knew coaches of the highest quality like Warren would be in big demand. Sacking Gareth Jenkins so quickly had not been something I relished. I had a high regard for him and liked him as a man, but we had to make a statement to Wales and the world that we were serious about recovering our position in the global game. Letting Gareth go immediately was a brutal necessity. I knew straight away that Warren was our man. I had spoken to him on the phone the week before, and he said he would meet us at the airport. He has incredibly high emotional intelligence, an awareness of people and situations. There is a perception that he is hard and driven, given his winning mentality, but he is also sensitive. What struck me at that first meeting was that he used the word legacy: he was concerned about the shape he would leave Wales in. Stability was also something he stressed. He stressed that it was not about one man and said that if he became our next head coach he would look to bring in Shaun Edwards and Robert Howley to his management team. We were all struck by his honesty as well as his professionalism.'

Gatland was quoted in *Wales on Sunday* that weekend as saying that the appeal of coaching Wales was diminished by the frequency with which the position became vacant. 'Every coach understands that results mean everything in professional sport, especially in the United Kingdom, but there's no point in merely toppling the coach every time the results don't go to plan,' he said. 'That has been one of the problems in Wales when you look at the number of coaches they have gone through in recent years. That is not going to give any candidate a feeling of confidence or security and might even put some people off. Any coaching position with an international side in the top eight nations is always going to be an attractive proposition. Coaching is all about rising to challenges, and the Wales job is bound to be viewed as a very appealing challenge around the world.' And he added: 'People shouldn't be too optimistic in the first year, whoever becomes national coach. That person is going to need a lot of support and help to ensure there is long-term development. I'd like to think they will give the new man a chance to make a difference. He will need the full support of the union and the nation to provide him with confidence – as will the team. It can't always be about winning tournaments. There has to be room and time for coaches and teams to develop and progress to a point where they punch at or above their weight.'

The WRU trio returned to Wales knowing the name of the man they would recommend to succeed Jenkins but were slightly unnerved by the fact that Gatland said he would meet them again at the end of the month when he arrived for a stay in Britain. They feared someone else was tapping him up; Gatland had admitted that he had been approached at some time in the year by another international side and that May had said he would consider returning to Europe. His ambition of coaching the Super 14 side Waikato Chiefs had not been realised, and would not for at least a couple more years. He was not considered a contender to succeed Henry, but when Wales's interest in him became known he was sounded out about a Super 14 job as the head coach of Otago Highlanders. He was not prepared to move his family to Dunedin, arguing later that he would effectively see as much of his wife and children if he decamped to New Zealand's South Island as if he were based in Cardiff. 'I felt I had done my time overseas, cut my teeth there then come back home and had three seasons with Waikato which were pretty good,' he said. 'But there were not any other opportunities for me in New Zealand. I had already turned down one overseas job at international level that year, and I don't think it would have been right to have spurned another opportunity.'

When Jenkins was fired, Lewis said it was not a case of one man taking the blame for failure. The responsibility was collective, but there was no one keen to do any sharing. The figures at the union who had appointed Jenkins remained; some had been involved in the badly handled departure of Ruddock, whose going matched his arrival in 2004 when he was appointed to a job he had not applied for. Lewis had not been involved in either decision. Indeed, he owed his position to the hash the WRU made of the Ruddock affair, the culmination of which saw an emergency general meeting of member clubs, exasperated by a lack of clarity over the issue, pass a proposal to revive the position of group chief executive, which had not been filled since the resignation of David Moffett on health grounds at the end of 2005.

Lewis started work at the end of October 2006. His career until then had been in the entertainment industry, although it could be said that the goings-on at the WRU had never been less than entertaining. After gaining a degree in music, he started work as a presenter for Radio Tees and then Capital Radio before becoming the head of music at BBC Radio 1. In the 1990s, he moved into the business side of the industry, taking charge of two record companies before becoming the managing director and controller of Classic FM. In 2004, he was appointed the managing director of ITV Wales, from where he joined the WRU.

Whereas both Ruddock and Jenkins had been employed on two-year contracts, with neither seeing them out, Gatland was offered a four-year deal, the first time the union had committed itself to such a long contract since officials flew to Sydney in 1998 to persuade Graham Henry that his future lay in Wales. When Gatland came to Britain after the Auckland Airport interview, he stayed at Lewis's house near Wales's base in the Vale of Glamorgan. Lewis had reversed the policy of his predecessor Moffett, who cut staff and budgets in order to take control of a debt which was worth nearly £70 million, eventually managing to reorganise it. Lewis saw the national side as the means of expanding the union's business. The success of 2005 had been squandered, goodwill quickly turning into dismay and despair. Gatland's appointment was about restoring credibility on and off the pitch with the union's debt still hefty at £40 million.

If the WRU wanted toughness, Gatland delivered on his first day at work at the start of December, even if he were in Dubai watching Wales play in a world-ranking sevens tournament. In an interview with BBC Wales, he left his charges in no doubt about what lay in store for them. 'I will start off by saying to them, "Imagine there is a mirror – when you come off the field I want you to look into it and say, 'I tried really hard today.'" If someone gives everything, that is fine. At times in training, we will put them under some stress and pressure. I will try to break some players physically and mentally to find out how tough they really are, and I am going to let them know that I will be trying to break them. You have to replicate in training what happens during a match. You have to have intensity and put yourselves under pressure in training so when a game comes around everyone is prepared for it physically and mentally. We will at times make things harder in training than they will be in a match. There is no excuse for a player pulling on an international jersey and not dying for the cause; if he's holding something back, he does not deserve to be there. The players are going to be playing a style of rugby I hope they will find challenging.'

He had eight weeks to appoint his management team and prepare for the opening match of the Six Nations, against England at Twickenham, a ground where Wales had not won for 20 years and where their World Cup preparations had suffered an appalling start the previous August when, fielding a largely second- and third-string side, they were thrashed 62–5. It was not a stadium that held any ghosts for Gatland, who won three Premiership titles there with Wasps, along with the Heineken Cup. He had told Lewis in Auckland that if Wales defeated England, the Grand Slam would be on, and he did nothing to play down expectation in his first interview as the Wales head coach.

'The Six Nations is a confidence tournament,' he said. 'Win a couple of games and you can get another couple. Lose two and you find yourself against a wall with a hole to dig yourself out of. Twickenham could not come much tougher as an opening game, but I have been involved in a few games there with Wasps and had some good victories. I have a pretty good insight into a number of the England players. It will be a big ask, because Wales have not tasted success there for some time, but one of my aims for us in the next couple of years is to achieve things Wales have not managed for a long time. One is getting a result against England at Twickenham.'

A feature of the 2005 Grand Slam was the barriers Wales knocked down. Their opening game that year was against England in Cardiff, and it had been 12 years since the men in white had lost in the city. Wales had not won at Murrayfield for eight years, while their home record against

Ireland was astonishingly dismal, with the last victory occurring way back in 1983. It was four years since they had won an away fixture in the Six Nations. One by one, the historical obstacles fell, and as they did so Wales gathered a momentum that became irresistible.

In 2008, as well as facing a trip to Twickenham, where they had suffered five record defeats since their eight-point victory in 1988, they had not won in Dublin for eight years, while France had not lost at the Millennium Stadium in the Six Nations. And Wales had not won away in the championship since their last Grand Slam season. 'One of the reasons I took the job was that Wales were tenth in the rankings and had had a pretty average World Cup,' said Gatland. 'There was not too far to go below tenth. I saw the potential and the ability within the squad and realised that, with the security of knowing I would have a couple of years in the job, I could change things by putting structures in place and making a difference. The talent was there. It was a matter of finding the switch.'

2

....

BYRNE'S NIGHT

And no one shall work for money, and no one shall
work for fame, but each for the joy of working.

Rudyard Kipling

14 **JANUARY 2008. WARREN GATLAND HAS JUST**
announced his first Wales squad. It includes the
32-year-old flanker Martyn Williams, who had announced
his retirement from international rugby after Wales's exit
from the World Cup and who, the previous month, had said
that nothing would persuade him to change his mind. One
telephone call from Gatland found him ready for turning.
Shaun Edwards and Robert Howley had the previous day
been appointed assistant coaches to their former boss at
Wasps, Edwards in charge of defence and Howley with
responsibility for attack. Although Gatland had identified
them immediately as two of the men he wanted in his

management team, contract negotiations had taken time with Edwards, head coach at Wasps, and Howley, an assistant coach at Cardiff Blues.

Howley is sitting in a room at the Vale of Glamorgan hotel, completing a round of interviews that all started with the same question: what are Gatland and Edwards like? 'People are asking me if I am taking a gamble getting involved in international rugby so early in my coaching career,' says Howley, a former Wales scrum-half and captain who was forced to retire from playing through injury in 2004. 'Somebody even asked me whether I was prepared to be on the dole in nine months' time, because coaching Wales was a thankless job. My reply was that I knew Warren and Shaun and what they were capable of. I have seen at first hand their ability to motivate and create an environment of utter professionalism. Warren will challenge everyone, coaches and players. He is a man of integrity who inspires trust, and he brings a common-sense approach to playing and training. I think Wales supporters are in for some exciting times. I went to Wasps late in my career, and I really enjoyed my time there under him and Shaun. It was all about how you responded to pressure. Shaun has a no-nonsense approach and gets the best out of players with his attention to detail, and I can guarantee that the players will never have come across anyone like him before: he is a one-off. Wales have conceded an average of more than three tries a match in recent times. I would not like to be in a Wales dressing-room after a match with Shaun if three tries have been leaked. These two guys will make a difference, and I am delighted to be involved.'

Gatland named the Ospreys' number 8 Ryan Jones as his first captain. Jones had been part of the 2005 Grand

Slam squad, starting the final three matches at blind-side flanker and making such an impact that he was called into the Lions squad in New Zealand that summer as a replacement, earning a Test place immediately. Captaincy had been a vexed issue for Gareth Jenkins. At the start of 2007, he had appointed the outside-half Stephen Jones as the skipper through to the World Cup, but as Wales opened their campaign with successive defeats, the Welsh media clamoured for James Hook, who had been picked at inside-centre, to play at outside-half, which he eventually did on the final weekend against England in Cardiff when Jones pulled out through injury. Wales avoided the whitewash and wooden spoon that day, and while Jones was to regain the number 10 jersey in the World Cup, Gareth Thomas was appointed the captain for the tournament. When Wales played South Africa in November 2007, less than two weeks before Gatland started work, the caretaker coach Nigel Davies gave the prop Gethin Jenkins the armband. He felt that Wales needed a forward to lead the side, and while Gatland did not agree with his choice, he shared the sentiment.

Ryan Jones returned from the Lions tour to New Zealand as one of the few players to enhance his reputation, but, symptomatic of the ill-fortune that dogged Wales after the Grand Slam, it was to be more than a year before he played international rugby again after having a shoulder operation. He played in the 2007 Six Nations, and it seems curious to reflect, after the way he led by example in 2008, that supporters were calling on Jenkins to drop him after the early defeats to Ireland and Scotland. 'It has been difficult for me to carry the ball with the amount of possession we have had,' Jones said at the time. 'People are saying that I have been anonymous, but I have been through the tapes, and I am happy with my work rate. I just have not had many opportunities.' He would have gone to the World Cup, but he suffered a shoulder injury in training the month before the tournament started and had to pull out. He returned to action in January 2008 and admitted he was surprised when he received a call from Gatland, asking him to captain Wales in the Six Nations.

'Warren's call marked a special day for me,' said Jones, who had been appointed as the Ospreys' captain at the beginning of the season. 'I had had another roller-coaster year, but being given the honour of leading your country makes all the pain worthwhile. It took me all of three seconds to accept, and I have felt ten feet tall ever since. I am in a privileged position, and it is a great job to have. People talk about it being a poisoned chalice, but those things are out of your control. It is difficult to deal with the expectation, because I am just a normal guy who happens to be good at rugby. The World Cup campaign was disappointing, but we have got to shake off the hangover and move on. We have a new management team, and it is a new era for Wales. Warren will create a pretty uncompromising environment, and it is up to the players to deliver.'

Gatland said that he had considered a number of players for the role. He ruled out Stephen Jones and Dwayne Peel because they faced intense competition for their places from Hook and Mike Phillips respectively. He singled out the second row Alun Wyn Jones and the flanker Jonathan Thomas as potential future captains, but said, 'Ryan is fit again and playing well. His ability on the pitch is unquestionable, and he has the necessary experience to fill the captaincy role, having been involved with the Lions. He has not hit his potential 100 per cent yet, having not long returned from injury, but he will be on top of his game by the time we face England.'

The biggest call made by Gatland was the one to Martyn Williams, the player of the Six Nations in 2005. 'I felt we had a lack of experience in his position of open-side flanker,' said Gatland. 'I saw him as the missing part of the jigsaw, and I gave him a ring. I told him he could tell me to bugger off, and I would respect that, but I said that I intended to create an environment based on hard work that he would be happy in. He asked for a weekend to think about it and called me back to say that he would make himself available. I was more than happy with that decision.' Fittingly, it was Williams who was to round off the Grand Slam success, scoring the final try against France at the Millennium Stadium to cap an evening in which he had shown why Gatland had been so keen to get him on board.

Yet the previous November, after a Man of the Match display for Cardiff Blues against Bristol in the Heineken Cup group match at the Arms Park, Williams was adamant that nothing and no one would coax him out of international retirement. 'I had made the decision at the start of 2007, and when I returned from the World Cup I thought I had done everything I could and did not have any targets left,' he said. 'I started to have second thoughts when I heard that Warren Gatland was taking over. I knew he would look to bring Shaun with him, and I fancied the prospect of working with them. I was willing my phone to ring. You think of Wasps and you picture a physical side which is intimidating to play against. There is a real feeling of excitement in the squad, and the fact that Warren and Shaun know a number of the England players well can help give us an extra edge at

Twickenham.' At the end of the championship, he reflected on his change of mind. 'I am probably showing my age, but Shaun was a great hero of mine. I was into rugby league in a big way, and he was an incredible player. Working with him has been an eye-opener, and you cannot quantify the difference he has made to us. There is a misconception about him that he raves and rants, but he is just someone with a seamless wealth of knowledge. Every week in training we do something specific to the game we are playing. We do not go through a drill for the sake of it. He is a winner, and we have fed off that.'

The return of Williams also showed the tough side to Gatland, who, when he arrived in Wales, stressed the importance of keeping what went on in the squad in-house. So, when Williams's about-turn was revealed in a Welsh newspaper before Gatland had had the chance to make the announcement publicly, he resolved to track down the source of the leak, discovering that it had not come from any of his players. He gathered them in the team room and wrote a telephone number on a board. No one, he told them, was to call the number while they were in camp. And, for the first time in years, there were to be no leaks ahead of team announcements. The players were left guessing when it came to selection and so were reporters.

Gatland's first squad contained only one uncapped player, the Cardiff wing/full-back Jamie Roberts. Ten players who were involved in the World Cup were omitted, including Gareth Thomas, who had become the first Welsh international to reach 100 caps when he led the side against Fiji in Nantes, and the veteran flanker Colin Charvis. Almost lost in the hubbub over the arrival of Edwards and the return of Williams was the presence of the centre Gavin Henson in the squad, another totemic figure from 2005 who had not started a Six Nations match since. Henson had come to personify the decline of Wales since the victory over Ireland three years before had secured Wales's first Grand Slam for twenty-seven years. A combination of injuries, suspension, the disapproval of some teammates after he published his autobiography at the end of 2005 and a collective failure to understand an enigmatic individual led to him becoming a peripheral figure. He was dropped from the Wales squad two weeks before the thirty for the World Cup in France had to be announced after reporting back to training with low fitness levels. It seemed the latest in a line of unnecessary humiliations, even if it was easy to understand why Gareth Jenkins had made the announcement early so that when he unveiled the squad the absence of Henson would not overshadow the campaign that would determine whether the coach held on to his job.

Jenkins had become exasperated during the 2007 Six Nations when constantly asked about Henson. The player might have been absent from the squad, but he haunted the Vale of Glamorgan Hotel. Jenkins had considered him as a full-back for the opening game against Ireland in Cardiff, and the Ospreys agreed to play him in the position that January. Henson did not have his best game and was left out of the 22 by Jenkins, subsequently ruled out of contention by injury. Henson returned for the summer tour to Australia, making an impact from the bench in the two Tests, but he was an outsider looking in. He was chosen in the centre for the November 2007 friendly against the World Cup holders South Africa in what was clearly a pre-emptive strike by Gatland, who had been warned that he would have to get to grips with a group of players who had been powerful during the Ruddock and Jenkins eras.

Henson's recall gave out a dual signal: Gatland was showing from the outset who was boss, and he was recognising that, given the relatively small pool of talent that Wales had to choose from, it was folly to ignore someone of the Ospreys' centre's ability. Gatland appreciated, too, that some players needed to be handled differently. The stick did not work with Henson, someone who gave off an air of detachment but who needed to feel wanted. His celebrity lifestyle had counted against him, and the previous month he had been charged after he and a group of friends were accused of drunken, rowdy antics on a train after he had helped the Ospreys defeat Harlequins in the EDF Energy Cup. However, the case against him was dropped before it came to court, and he started with a clean slate under his fifth coach in little more than six years as an international player. 'Shaun and I specialise in this kind of player,' said Gatland. 'We had a joke about it at Wasps and called ourselves the "Home for Wayward Players". A number of guys came to us with reputations, but they fitted in really well. If they are happy and know the boundaries, you do not get any problems with them. I am not looking to make an issue of it. I think Gavin has matured. He's got a young family now, and I'd like nothing better than for him to concentrate on rugby and put the criticisms behind him. Let's start afresh. I first saw him play for the Under-20s, and if there was one player who stood out as a bit special, it was Gavin. He was big, physical, quick, composed and he had a huge boot. There would be no better achievement than if he became a major contender for the Lions in 2009. I don't want players to be clones of each other. There are team protocols, such as turning up on time and being good with the media, and if you step out of line, you are going to get a kick up the backside, but I am pretty forgiving of players who get back on the rails.'

Gatland did not talk down his new charges and was confrontational in the build-up to the Twickenham encounter. He questioned England's selection of Iain Balshaw at full-back, saying he had been unimpressed with the player when he had watched him appearing for Gloucester, and he mocked the Rugby Football Union for letting Shaun Edwards slip away over the Severn Bridge. 'When it came out publicly that I was keen on getting Shaun, England offered him the Saxons job,' he said. 'They did that so that they could say they tried to hold on to him, but I am just surprised that he has not been tapped into at all by England, and not just as a defence coach, because he has so much to contribute.' And he also had a dig at the RFU for only rehiring the coach who took the side to an unlikely World Cup final, Brian Ashton, on a reported one-year rolling contract. 'That does not offer a huge amount of confidence,' he said. 'As a player, I would be asking how long Ashton was going to be there. If England were not prepared to give him more than a year, why did they not make a change?'

Ashton's future would become a recurring theme after Wales's victory at Twickenham. Even when England finished the Six Nations with their most complete performance, at home to Ireland, attention centred on whether Ashton would be around for the summer tour to New Zealand. Gatland had played up his side's prospects against England at the beginning of the week of the Twickenham trip in an interview with *The Guardian*: 'One of the mistakes England made after winning the World Cup in 2003 was keeping so many of those players for an 18-month period when they needed to develop new players and stick with them. Surely Brian would love to be able to do the same thing and pick a squad of younger, talented players and be able to develop them over a period towards the next World Cup? If you look at the England squad now, it is a mixture, with players who are on their last legs but who perhaps have the experience to get you the results for now. I don't think it is the best thing for English rugby, because they might end up going through the same cycle of disappointment as they did five years ago. It looks to me like they have gone for the same old pattern.'

Wales had not had such a direct speaker as head coach since another New Zealander, Graham Henry, had arrived in the summer of 1998. 'England's squad does not hold any fears for me, and my players should not have any in believing that they can get a result there,' he said after announcing his first team. It contained thirteen Ospreys, the largest representation from one side since Cardiff supplied ten sixty years before, a campaign which also opened away to England. The wing Mark Jones and Martyn Williams were the exceptions, prompting one poster to BBC Wales's interactive forum to write, 'I can't believe what Gatland has done. I've instantly lost all respect for the guy.' While many things changed in Welsh rugby, one aspect remained the same: tribalism. The post ignored the fact that Gatland had the squad together for less than two weeks. His team for Twickenham contained a strong element of familiarity, and all the backs bar one were used to the blitz defence. He had helped out at an Ospreys' training session the week before, and the performance of the region in cross-border tournaments provided him with a short cut to Twickenham. Familiarity bred content.

The Ospreys were the most successful of Wales's four regions. They had reached the quarter-finals of the Heineken Cup, along with Cardiff Blues, and they were the only Welsh representatives in the semi-finals of the EDF Energy Cup. They were the home of players such as Ryan Jones, Henson, Hook, Shane Williams, Alun Wyn Jones and Jonathan Thomas, but there was one overriding reason why a surfeit of their players was chosen: the blitz defence system favoured by Edwards. The Ospreys were the only region to operate it. The previous year, Gareth Jenkins had looked to implement a blitz defence and asked the other three regions – the Blues, Llanelli Scarlets and Newport Gwent Dragons – if they would adopt it. He met with three refusals but pressed ahead anyway. Some of the tries Wales conceded in the World Cup were due to some players rushing up in defence slower than others. Edwards maintained that Wales would not be blitzing against England because, with less than two weeks to prepare for the game, there had not been enough time to familiarise the players with the system. Given the preponderance of Ospreys, no one believed him.

The team was largely made up of players who had been involved in the World Cup campaign. Ryan Jones and Henson were the exceptions, along with the full-back Lee Byrne, who had played in the August friendly at Twickenham only to be left out of the squad for France. The full-back position was vacant following Gatland's decision not to pick Gareth Thomas, and Byrne was not a universally popular choice. He had started in three championship matches in 2006, but his only appearance the following year came in Paris. He was one of the very few Wales players to emerge from the 57-point defeat to England in credit, but it was not enough to get him to the World Cup. He had a reputation for being inconsistent and occasionally lacking in concentration, but he had been enjoying a successful season with the Ospreys. 'The big thing for me was that Warren came in and said he would judge players on form,' he said. 'He watched the Ospreys a few times, and when I was named in the squad, he told me what he wanted from me. I just had to go out in training and prove myself to the coaches.' Byrne summed up a difference the regime had made later in the tournament, after Wales had secured the Triple Crown in Dublin. 'I did not do anything exceptional against Ireland,' he said. 'I don't feel I had a great game, but a couple of years ago I would have been happy with my performance. Warren and Shaun make you push the bar higher, and I am aware now just how much more I have to learn. The World Cup is gone and forgotten as far as I am concerned. I believe that things happen for a reason, and I was not meant to go to France. It gave me the kick up the backside I needed, because I knew I was good enough to compete at the top level.' Byrne also received some advice from Shaun Edwards. 'I had heard that Lee was a player who got over-aroused before a game,' said the defence coach. 'I suffered from the same thing as a player and was often too fired up before we went out on to the pitch. I gave him a tip that had worked for me: read a book, any book. He said it had helped him at Twickenham, and it is something I have recommended to a few players in my time.'

As it had been in 2005, the key to the Grand Slam was the victory over England. Wales won despite playing their worst half of rugby during the entire tournament. They trailed 16–6 at the interval; the deficit would have been greater had the wing Paul Sackey not been stopped on the line by the hooker Huw Bennett, who got his arm underneath the ball. England had a prime scoring opportunity at the end of the half when they had two attacking lineouts five yards from the Wales line. The forward defence held firm against a series of drives, even if the replacement flanker Alix Popham was fortunate not to receive a yellow card after killing the ball at the breakdown, an act of indiscipline which was to earn him a public rebuke from Gatland, and he did not feature in the match squad for the rest of the campaign. Another element of fortune was the knee injury to the replacement flanker Tom Rees as England pressed for their second try. They had already lost their other open-side wing forward, Lewis Moody, earlier in the half with an injury that was to end his season and were forced to play the second 40 minutes with an unbalanced back row after bringing on the second row Ben Kay.

Wales were relieved to hear the interval whistle, and as they made their way to the dressing-room the odds on their winning the Grand Slam would have been the same as on an England victory against Australia at Headingley in the 1981 Ashes series when Graham Dilley joined Ian Botham at the wicket. England had made a strong start at Twickenham, but lost Moody in addition to the wing David Strettle, who was injured after making a forty-five-yard break, around or through seven tacklers, into the Wales twenty-five that came to grief when he took the wrong option, while Jonathan Thomas also departed inside the opening fifteen minutes after ducking into a Jonny Wilkinson tackle and getting caught on the face. Mark Jones was also in a daze for a few minutes after receiving an inadvertent blow on the head from Strettle's replacement, the imposing Lesley Vainikolo, but quickly learned that 'seeing stars' was no excuse as far as Edwards was concerned for not taking his place in the defensive line.

Gatland had talked before the match of Wales becoming stronger in the tackle area, but they were turned over six times in the opening twenty-five minutes. The lack of preparation time with a new coaching regime looked to be a telling factor, with players uncertain when to kick or run, and they were repeatedly caught out at restarts. Yet for all their dominance, England scored only one try: Wilkinson floated a cross-field kick for Vainikolo, who beat Mark Jones to the ball and, as he fell to the ground, weighted his pass for the supporting Toby Flood. It was to become the only time in the tournament that an attacking strategy resulted in a try against Wales. Gatland did not rant and rave at his players during the interval, telling them to respect the ball and go out and play.

Few of the team were old enough to remember Wales's previous victory at Twickenham in 1988. The wing Adrian Hadley scored two tries in an 11–3 success, the first leg of what turned out to be Wales's first Triple Crown for nine years. The then coach Tony Gray had gone into the match without a recognised full-back after leaving out Paul Thorburn in favour of Anthony Clement, who had played almost all his rugby at outside-half. Gray, who had guided Wales to third in the World Cup the previous year, wanted his side to play with freedom and felt that the only way to show his players that they were not taking to the field limping was to remove the crutch of a goal-kicker.

The following years had seen a series of humiliations inflicted on Wales as England started their rise up the world rankings. A then record 34–6 defeat in 1990 prompted the resignation of John Ryan as coach; England piled up 60 points in 1998, 46 in 2000, 50 in 2002, 47 in 2006 and 62 in 2007. It was a sequence of scores and results that showed how far Wales had fallen since their heyday in the 1970s, but to Gatland and Edwards Twickenham was a ground that held only fond memories. 'We knew it was the defining game in our season,' said Edwards. 'Our next two matches were against Scotland and Italy at home, and we expected to win those. When we arrived at Twickenham, our goal was to become the Six Nations champions, but we did not test England in the first half. We kicked the ball too much, and we did not have any balance in our game. We were just glad to get into the break only ten points behind, because it meant we were still in there. It could have been a lot worse.'

England increased their lead to 13 points at the start of the second half with a Jonny Wilkinson penalty and had a prime opportunity to put the game beyond Wales. England kicked a penalty to touch five yards from the Wales line, in the corner where Robert Howley had won the 2004 Heineken Cup for Wasps by pouncing while the Toulouse full-back Clément Poitrenaud dithered. They drove the lineout and were awarded another penalty, but this time Wilkinson opted to go for goal, a conservatism for which his team paid a high price.

England should have been on a high after reaching the World Cup final against all the odds, but the official review of the campaign had taken two months and amounted to a half-hearted vote of confidence in Brian Ashton and his coaching team. Player discontent had been voiced during the World Cup, culminating in critical remarks of the coaching team made by two veterans of the 2003 campaign, Lawrence Dallaglio and Mike Catt, extracts from which were published in newspapers the weekend after the final against South Africa.

The final had been a largely sterile affair. One of the players who provided some of the few moments of illumination, the centre Mathew Tait, did not make the 22 against Wales. He had been talked about as an option to Balshaw at full-back but was ruled out after struggling there for Newcastle at Leicester the week before the start of the Six Nations. Where Gray had been bold in 1988, and the Wales selectors 21 years before – when they gave the 19-year-old Keith Jarrett, a centre by preference, what turned out to be a history-making 19-point debut at full-back against England at Cardiff Arms Park despite a first appearance there for Newport at Newbridge the week before that was so shaky that he was moved back into the midfield for the second half – England opted for experience in the shape of Balshaw. Gatland picked up on it, and Balshaw was to provide the moment that ended Wales's 20-year drought in the English capital.

It was the only match in which the wing Shane Williams failed to score a try, but he proved to be the catalyst for Wales's comeback at Twickenham. Nine minutes of the second half had gone when Wilkinson was penalised for holding on to the ball in Wales's twenty-five, although he had been dispossessed by Martyn Williams, an incident that marked the turning point at the breakdown; from then on it would be England who got turned over. Shane Williams took the penalty quickly and started a move that ended in England's 25. England were again caught out on fifty-three minutes when the centre Mike Tindall was tackled by Ryan Jones and Popham on Wales's ten-yard line. England's forwards were slow to arrive, and Wales were awarded the put-in at a scrum; two minutes later, Mike Phillips charged down his opposite number Andy Gomarsall's kick, and although Wilkinson gathered the ball, he was pounced on by four Wales forwards and conceded a scrum from which Henson charged into the midfield and earned his side a penalty when the flanker James Haskell failed to roll away.

Wales gained position after England had been in possession, and that was to become a feature of their campaign. Hook kicked the penalty to bring his side back to 19–9 down, and the momentum was now with the visitors. Simon Shaw won a turnover for England, but Gomarsall passed the ball behind Balshaw. Byrne hacked it into England's 25, and Balshaw, under pressure from Ryan Jones and Henson, conceded a penalty for not releasing that Hook converted. England were leading 19–12 but hanging on, and the loss of Mike Tindall, who suffered a damaged liver after trying to ankle-tap Byrne, destabilised their midfield. Wilkinson became his side's one outfield player of real experience, but the player whose extra-time drop goal won the 2003 World Cup final made a mistake that was so out of character that you needed to watch a replay of the incident to confirm it was him.

Wilkinson received a pass from Gomarsall on his own ten-yard line. The Wales defence had fanned out in a line, and no one was charging at him. He had ample time to put boot to ball, and, with his side in desperate need of territory, a relieving kick seemed the obvious call. Instead, he threw out a long pass to Danny Cipriani, Tindall's 20-year-old replacement who was making his international debut. The ball went over Cipriani's head and bounced inside England's 25. Cipriani managed to retrieve it but was scragged by Tom Shanklin. Gethin Jenkins, Duncan Jones and Ian Gough were the first forwards to arrive, and Wales were awarded a scrum. Wilkinson said in his newspaper column the following Monday that he felt obliged to pass because Wales players were bearing down on him. He said it was the execution rather than the idea that was at fault, but a freeze-frame of the tape at the moment he received the ball showed no opponent within ten yards of him.

Wales took play through six phases after the scrum before they went blind on the left-hand side. Hook received the ball and, feinting inside and out in almost the same moment, bought the space for the supporting Byrne to run through and score. Hook's conversion brought the scores level, and England were still collecting themselves when Mike Phillips returned the restart with a kick into England territory. Balshaw fielded the ball and dithered slightly before opting to punt. Phillips had chased hard, just as Wales had worked on in training, and charged down the clearance. Gethin Jenkins picked up and found the supporting Martyn Williams, who fed the looping Phillips for Wales's second try in as many minutes. Hook's conversion gave Wales a 26–19 lead; they had scored 20 unanswered points in 13 minutes. A television camera panned to Gatland and Edwards sitting in the stand. They remained impassive: there were still ten minutes to go, time for England to lose control of the ball yet again, Gomarsall conceding a scrum after being caught in possession in his own twenty-five. Wales used the position to run down the clock with a series of pick-and-drives. It was a tactic used by England in years past, and by the time the men in white got hold of the ball and moved away from their own line, the countdown clock had reached zero, and the final whistle would sound the next time the ball went dead.

Gatland and Edwards were caught on camera again, this time sporting grins. 'I turned to Shaun with a few minutes to go and asked if we should show some emotion and jump up and down if we held on to the lead,' said Gatland. 'As we chatted on the coach coming to Twickenham, we reflected that it had been a happy ground for us. I was disappointed with the start we made, but the players hung in there, crucially holding England out either side of the interval. As the game went on, we got stronger, and the guys gained a bit of self-belief and confidence. I spoke to Brian Ashton after the game, and he was wondering how they had lost while I was trying to figure out how we had won. It is a good start, but we still have a lot of work to do. The raw material is there, and when we get it right we will be a very good side.'

Gatland had said before the game that he would not be afraid to use his bench, and six minutes into the second half with his side thirteen points down he brought on Shanklin to replace Sonny Parker in the centre and Gethin Jenkins to pack down at tight-head prop in place of Adam Jones. Shanklin and Jenkins had been ever-presents in the 2005 campaign, the latter scoring the opening try in the final match against Ireland and Shanklin going on to create the decisive try in the second half that afternoon. Parker had been chosen to start against England because of his familiarity with Edwards's defensive system, but Wales were in a position where they needed to attack, and, as Gatland acknowledged, the use of a second row as a replacement for the open-side Tom Rees after the interval had left England less mobile in the back row. Parker had seen little of the ball, apart from the restarts when Wilkinson singled him out, but Shanklin made a difference as he resumed his midfield partnership with Henson that had been a feature of the 2005 season.

Wales won the second half 20–3 in what was to become another recurring theme of their Six Nations campaign. Their second-period score against Scotland was 20–9 and 20–6 against France; it was 34–0 against Italy and 13–6 against Ireland in Dublin. The second-half aggregate was 107–24, whereas the interval score in the five matches added up to 41–42, with England and Ireland enjoying half-time leads. The two tries Wales conceded both came before the break, and they did not concede one point in the final quarter of any of their opening three matches before Ireland mustered six and France three. It was a tribute to the training regime imported from Wasps by Gatland and Edwards.

The players had been used to training sessions dragging on for up to two hours. Concentration often wavered and focus became blurred, but Gatland and Edwards, adopting the model they had introduced at Wasps, opted for the short, sharp shock treatment. Sessions sometimes only lasted 40 minutes as the coaches looked to replicate the optimum time the ball is in play during an international. Every Wales player who was interviewed during the build-up to Twickenham used the same word: intensity. 'I have never worked so hard in my life,' said Shane Williams. 'The World Cup showed that when it comes to using the ball, we are up there with the top sides, but our defence was not good enough, and Shaun has really put us through our paces. We need to become harder to break down without compromising our attacking flair. Shaun is very intense and emotional, and he has given me special defence sessions. He has had me working with the back row and the centres. We battered hell out of each other, and Shaun joined in.'

Hook revealed that when Gatland had helped out at the Ospreys before their Heineken Cup match against Gloucester at the Liberty Stadium, his presence had put everybody on edge. 'He worked with the forwards and really got stuck in,' said Hook. 'There were a few scuffles among the boys, and he got them to show how much they wanted it. There has been a greater intensity to training with Wales than we have been used to, and we now have a much sharper focus.'

The only Englishman smiling after the match was Shaun Edwards, and he led the singing in the dressing-room afterwards. He surprised everyone with a rendition of the Drifters' 1964 hit 'Saturday Night at the Movies'. 'I just wanted the team to have a song, and it was the only one I knew the words to,' he said. 'We had just beaten England in their own back yard, and everyone was just sat down in the dressing-room. I started singing and everyone else joined in, and the song has become a theme for us now. The players did look at me a bit strangely at first, but you have to celebrate your victories, and there is no better way to do that than singing a song.' A bond had been struck. James Bond. Never say never again.

3

···

BENCHMARK

> No bird soars too high, if he soars
> with his own wings.
>
> *William Blake*

4 **FEBRUARY 2008. THE WALES TEAM HOTEL IS EERILY** quiet as the media arrive for a briefing with selected players. The celebrations after the England victory did not survive that night's journey from Twickenham. It marked a contrast to previous years when success against England was seen as a glorious one-off, affirmation of a successful season. 'We can always go back to beating England,' commented the then team manager Clive Rowlands after Wales had lost 49–6 to New Zealand in the 1987 World Cup semi-final. It was, at the time, the heaviest defeat suffered by the men in red, but it was, in the coming years, to become the norm rather than the exception. The game was changing, with the

45

World Cup the accelerant. The dawn of the professional era might have been eight years away, but the likes of the All Blacks, soon to be followed by England, were already anticipating it. When Wales beat England in 1989, they failed to win any of their next eight Five Nations matches. After they started the 1993 championship by defeating England 10–9 at the National Stadium, three defeats followed. The gush of emotion that greeted the unlikely successes drained Wales mentally. There was no danger of that under Warren Gatland.

The following day, he was due to announce his team to face Scotland that Saturday. He was already committed to one change, because the second row Alun Wyn Jones had sustained ankle-ligament damage in the dying minutes at Twickenham, but by focusing on Wales's no-show in the first-half as much as their comeback after the interval, the head coach had laid the foundations for further alteration. The first time he met the squad, he told them that they would be judged by how they performed in training as much as their displays on the field. He would provoke a reaction out of them, and a negative one would prompt a return to their regions. 'Everyone is aware that, although we beat England, there are a number of areas we have to work on,' said the prop Gethin Jenkins. 'What Twickenham showed was that we had improved in an area where we were weak last year: closing a game out. We failed to make the World Cup quarter-finals because we did not boss the final ten minutes against Fiji after taking the lead, but at Twickenham we held on to the ball at the end after getting our noses in front and stopped them from getting back into the game. Saturday will be another test: it is easy when you are the underdogs, as we were at Twickenham, but we will be the favourites against Scotland. It is a completely different proposition, and we have to show that we can deal with expectation.'

Even though England reached the World Cup final, Scotland were the only home union side to return home from the tournament anxious for their head coach to sign a new contract. Ireland, who had given Eddie O'Sullivan a new four-year deal just before the squad left for France, announced they would conduct an exhaustive review into the campaign after failing to reach the quarter-finals; England were to pursue the same course, while Wales had already said their farewells to Gareth Jenkins. Scotland had reached the last eight, where they were knocked out by Argentina in Paris. Under their head coach Frank Hadden, they had become a well-prepared team, hard to break down if offering little threat when in possession. They had been drawn in the same pool as New Zealand, and Hadden had decided to field a largely reserve team against the All Blacks in Edinburgh, keeping his leading players back for the quarter-final decider against Italy in Saint-Étienne six days later. It earned him a large measure of opprobrium, and the New Zealand match proved a tedious turn-off for television viewers with little to distinguish the two sets of jerseys. As a commentator said, the All Blacks were the ones with the ball.

Hadden was unrepentant and was rewarded with a narrow victory over Italy before Scotland gave Argentina more to think about than Ireland had. They started the Six Nations for once blessed with a tinge of optimism. Their first opponents were France at Murrayfield, a fixture the Scots had won two years before. The French were under new management, with Marc Lièvremont taking over as head coach from Bernard Laporte and promising to take the team back in time. Laporte had been fixated with winning the 2007 World Cup, so much so that France under him became England in blue: organised, disciplined, functional and, well, boring. The free enterprise that had characterised Les Bleus through the years, the flourish and the elan with which they played the game, had been replaced by an approach based on the elimination of mistakes. Ultimately, it failed: France lost the opening match in the World Cup to Argentina in Paris at the Stade de France, unable to chase the game, and their tactical timidity was rewarded by defeat to England in the semi-final at the same venue. They were even denied the consolation of finishing third when Argentina reminded the crowd at the Parc des Princes what handling, running rugby looked like as they sent Laporte to his government job crushed and bowed.

Lièvremont was taking a long-term view. He was a surprise choice to succeed Laporte, having just taken Dax back into the top division in France. He had played in the 1999 World Cup finals and had coached France at Under-21 level between 2003 and 2005, but his relative coaching inexperience was expected to count against him. Yet if his appointment was unpredictable, it was symbolic, because Lièvremont vowed to restore France's traditional values. Under Laporte, the France team had mostly been culled from clubs who had been successful in the Heineken Cup – Toulouse, Stade Français and Biarritz, with a sprinkling from Clermont Auvergne and Perpignan – but Lièvremont determined to exploit fully one of the advantages France had over every other country in the world, with the exception of England: a deep player base. Over the course of the championship, clubs such as Dax, Montpelier, Auch and

Albi were represented in the match 22. Lièvremont's policy of change, both in personnel and tactics, was predicted to take time, and Edinburgh on a cold early February afternoon was not expected to provide evidence of a French Revolution, especially against a Scotland side armed with something approaching confidence.

The result was a resounding 27–6 France victory. From being secure in his job, Hadden found himself under pressure when he arrived in Cardiff. Scotland had failed to score a try for the third match in four and, while France had enjoyed an element of fortune with close refereeing calls going their way, looked a side devoid of ideas. 'I am glad there is only a six-day turnaround before Wales, because we want to get things out and put things right,' said the Scotland outside-half Chris Paterson, who had surprisingly started the match against France on the bench. 'There will be some fire in our bellies.' Scotland had humbled Wales at Murrayfield a year before, dominating up front, and the afternoon proved to be seminal for Gareth Jenkins. The media criticism he received in the following days never let up, and the man dubbed the people's champion when he took over in May 2006 found himself sucked into a vortex of despair that he was never able to fight his way out of.

Wales were wary of the rebound factor, but it was always going to be a match that would be a test of how they used possession rather than how they defended. Gatland and Edwards had used words such as discipline, focus and concentration in their few weeks with the players, but they were also conscious not to destroy the one element of Wales's game that was a strength in the World Cup: attack. 'People keep asking me if we are going to become a defensively minded team,' said Edwards. 'We will when the opposition have the ball. But when we have the ball, we will be an attack-minded team. Wales had a great side in the 1970s, one which is renowned for its flair, but while we all remember the great tries they scored and the sweeping length-of-the-field moves, we forget all the hard work that went on behind the success. I spoke to a few people who had been involved in that era, including Gareth Edwards and John Taylor, and they said the team was built on a rock-solid defence. There were games last year when Wales conceded nearly 40 points. You do not have to be Einstein to work out that it is going to be very difficult to win matches if you are giving that many points away.'

One interested observer was the former Scotland wing Kenny Logan, who could claim to be bipartisan given that he was married to the television presenter Gabby Logan, the daughter of the former Wales football manager Terry Yorath. Logan was at Wasps when Edwards and then Gatland arrived. 'Shaun is amazing,' he said. 'When I first met him, I thought he was off his head and needed shooting. Within six weeks, I had come to respect him as much as any coach I had ever met. The Wales players will find that under Warren and Shaun they work harder than they ever have done in their careers. Warren is astute, refined and quiet, a good listener. He very rarely goes off his head, but when he does, watch out. Shaun is a different character: he can be quiet, and he thinks deeply before he says things to players, but when he is coaching he is in a different world. I do not think there is anyone in the world who coaches as he does. He is so enthusiastic he seems to play the game with you, and that enthusiasm rubs off on players. He will say what is in his head and deliver those thoughts straight to your face. You don't want to let him down, because you like and respect him. That is the difference for players with good coaches: you do not want to play for the ones who do not know what they are talking about. In Warren, Shaun and Rob Howley, Wales have men who have been there and done it.'

Gatland wanted his players to be ruthless – not to react to success with satisfaction but to treat it as another step climbed. He showed his ruthless side by making five changes from the twenty-two who had been involved at Twickenham. Ian Evans replaced the injured Alun Wyn Jones in the second row, while the back rower Alix Popham was dumped from the bench for giving away too many penalties against England. He had replaced Jonathan Thomas and played all bar the opening quarter of an hour of the match. He had not been on the pitch for a minute when he became involved in a spat with the England hooker Mark Regan on the touchline that went unnoticed by the match officials. It did not even amount to handbags – raised fists and voices – but it was conducted right underneath where Gatland was sitting. 'I was very disappointed with the penalties Alix gave away,' said Gatland. 'He was fortunate not to receive a yellow card, and he has things to work on to compete at this level.' Popham remained in the larger squad but was not to figure in a match 22 again in the Six Nations. The Gloucester number 8 Gareth Delve took his place among the replacements.

In the backs, Mark Jones was dropped for making some defensive errors. He was the only one of the starting backs at Twickenham who'd had to take a crash course in the art of the blitz defence and admitted that there were times when he'd had to remind himself to move up quickly rather than drift wide. Jones was replaced by the uncapped Jamie

Roberts, a 21-year-old medical student who had originally been chosen in the squad as a full-back. The former Wales captain Mike Hall had said after the England victory that he thought having both Shane Williams and Mark Jones on the wings, two players renowned for their speed rather than their size, increased the risk of Wales being stripped of the ball when they moved it wide. Roberts had the physique of a loose forward and was less than impressed when he read the official handout that put his height at 6 ft 3 in. 'I am 6 ft 6 in.,' he said, confirming that he weighed in at 16 st. 10 lb. 'At the start of the season, I could only dream of this moment, and it feels slightly surreal. I have to get my feet back on to the ground and make sure I enjoy the occasion, not let it get to me.'

The other change came in the centre, where Tom Shanklin replaced Sonny Parker, while the fit-again scrum-half Dwayne Peel displaced Gareth Cooper on the bench. 'It is not a question of the coaches being ruthless but picking what we feel is the best team for this match,' said Gatland, who had reduced the number of Ospreys in the side from 13 to 12, although 13 would start the match, with the Scotland wing Nikki Walker in his second season at the Liberty Stadium. 'When you beat England at Twickenham, you don't feel the need to make changes, but there are areas where we think we can improve. Scotland may be hoping that they find us in a complacent mood after such a great result, but nothing could be further from the truth. We enjoyed the win, but 24 hours later we were straight back to business. We know we have to improve, and if we are to get another result, we will have to put in a better performance. We have a squad of 28 players, and what we are saying to those who were not involved at Twickenham is that if they train well, they will have an opportunity. I have been impressed with Jamie Roberts and have told Mark Jones that there are a couple of areas he needs to work on: he conceded a couple of turnovers, and there are defensive aspects he has to pay attention to. What we are saying to players is that there are no guarantees. They have to perform.'

Gatland also had some advice for the outside-half James Hook. 'He has to be more accurate in his kicking. He put one out on the full against England, while a cross-kick put us under all sorts of pressure. He also needs to be more vocal and dominant in his demeanour. If he can improve in those areas, he will become world-class. He is an outside-half with a huge amount of potential and skill, and the fact he kicked all his goals at Twickenham was as important as anything. If Wales had kicked their goals against Fiji last September, they would have made the quarter-finals. I thought the craft he showed to create Lee Byrne's try, the footwork and sleight of hand, was just sensational. I think some of the players have been surprised at the amount of criticism we have made of a side that won at a place where they had not tasted success for 20 years, but you cannot just say to them, "Fantastic, well done, pat on the back, now let's train." You need to improve from week to week. If we do not point out faults, how are they going to get better?'

Hook received the observations with the same air of detachment he would show to an onrushing defender. 'A lot of the criticism was justified, because we did not play well in the first half at Twickenham. We made a number of errors, conceded silly penalties and let England into the game. We knew at the end that we had been slightly fortunate to win. A little criticism will not do us any harm, and we can look forward with confidence because of the way we came back in the second half when we did what we do best: kept the ball in hand and used our outside backs. England could not cope with it.'

The new regime was based on honesty, something that suited Gavin Henson, whose candour had not made him a universally popular figure within the camp in the past. 'I think we only played well for ten minutes in total, but that was enough,' said Henson. 'We tend to make it hard for ourselves, and I had a feeling of déjà vu: in 2005 we played France in Paris and did not have a look-in in the first half before staging a comeback. I was struggling with a sore Achilles tendon in the opening half at Twickenham, and I was not sure if I would make it to the interval to get a pain-killing injection from the doctor. I did not want to come off, because I knew we would become stronger in the second half, and I did not want to miss out on that.'

In retrospect, even though Twickenham marked the greatest achievement of the 2008 Grand Slam campaign, it was probably the least impressive of Wales's five performances. The first half held little in the way of credit, other than resolute defending at the end of it, but the display reflected the relatively little time the new management team had had with their charges. As the campaign went on and understanding grew, Wales came to embody Gatland and Edwards more and more, even to the point of succumbing to the Wasps tradition of being slow starters. There was a period against Scotland when Wales slowly started to surrender the initiative, playing as if the game had already been won, and the visitors clawed their way back, despite labouring under the severe handicap of being almost completely devoid of any creative ability. What they were armed with was the unerring boot of Chris Paterson, who had not missed a kick at goal in an international match since a friendly against Ireland before the World Cup. And he was given plenty of practice before Gatland acted quickly and decisively by using his bench.

Straight talking was a feature of his regime, or should that be straight shouting? In his BBC online column, Shanklin wrote:

> I've never had a coach screaming in my face before, but do you know something? It's great. That's part of life under the new Wales coaching regime. Warren Gatland and Shaun Edwards are blunt, direct and say it as it is. They do not beat about the bush – they say it straight away. I could repeat some of the choice words that Shaun has used, but perhaps swearing is not the way to go in this column. Their approach may offend some people, but they said from the very start that they are not about picking on anyone – they are trying to help. They are probably trying to make us feel that as they take no prisoners off the field, we should take none on it, and it's really good. Screaming in your face is how Shaun gets his point across, and I think it is a great coaching style. People should have seen the effect he, Warren and the other coaches had on the team at Twickenham. It is a no-nonsense approach, and all the boys respect it.

Judgement was another keyword. It was something Wales had lacked during the World Cup despite the wealth of leadership experience that ran through the side. Their style was anarchic rather than free. 'We do not want to throw away what is called the Welsh style, but it is all about blending the free spirit with the basics,' said Gatland. 'We are working really hard on the set-pieces, contact area and defence.' What was notable about the second-half display at Twickenham was the increasing authority exerted by the half-backs, Mike Phillips and Hook. 'We were in a big hole at the break, and they were instrumental in our clambering out,' said Rob Howley. 'The game management in the last twenty-five minutes, especially the last ten, was outstanding. James appeared to grow ten feet tall, and you could tell he felt at ease. He made excellent decisions under pressure, while Mike read the game well at scrum-half. He touched the ball more than sixty times but made only five carries. He is a big, physical player who likes to take on opponents, but he waited for the gaps to open. We are not trying to restrict players but encourage them to make the right call at the right time. It's all about judgement.'

Phillips won his 29th cap against England, but more than half had come as a replacement, and his regular presence on the bench had earned him the nickname 'Splinters'. At the age of 25, he was on his third region, having started at Llanelli Scarlets then moving to Cardiff Blues before, in the summer of 2007, signing for the Ospreys, where he had to vie for a place with the former New Zealand scrum-half Justin Marshall. Like the flanker Jonathan Thomas, he was in the Wales side despite not holding down a regular place with his region, but he was not a player who lacked anything when it came to self-belief. Peel's injury had spared Gatland having to make a choice in the position at Twickenham, but Phillips was confident of getting the nod anyway. He had publicly voiced his disapproval during the World Cup of playing second fiddle to Peel. 'The last coaches were behind Dwayne in a big way,' he said. 'The new management team are open-minded, and this is a fresh start for me. I have been given the chance I wanted, and my destiny is in my own hands. There is a really positive mood about the place, and I feel much more part of the squad than I did before. We know as a team that our overall performance against England was not good enough, but we have a lot of talent, and, if we put certain things right, we can do well this year. I would like to be playing more for the Ospreys, but Justin is a great competitor, and I have learned a lot from him. I do not agree with those who say the move has held me back.'

If Phillips and Hook had been pivotal figures at Twickenham, it was their replacements who would take Wales home against Scotland. Phillips and Hook had helped create their side's opening try on 13 minutes when the scrum-half made a powerful surge after the Scotland full-back miscalculated a chip ahead. Wales, as they had done for their opening try at Twickenham, moved left, where Hook, with understated movement after Henson had straightened the line, put Byrne into space, and Shane Williams side-stepped his way over for his thirty-sixth international try, four short of Gareth Thomas's Wales record. Scotland had earlier taken the lead with a Paterson penalty after absorbing initial Welsh pressure and cashing in on a stray Hook pass, but they looked in trouble after 17 minutes when their second row Nathan Hines was sent to the sin-bin for clouting Byrne off the ball. Wales failed to make use of their one-man advantage, even when they had a series of scrums five yards from Scotland's line, a sequence which ended when the scrum-half Mike Blair dispossessed Ryan Jones. Wales only extended their lead with a Hook penalty after Hines had returned to the field, with Paterson quickly responding in kind.

Wales's 10–6 interval lead was a better return than they had managed at Twickenham, but Gatland looked anything but pleased as the television camera panned to the Wales management team shortly before the half-time whistle, and he went to the dressing-room armed with a message. It was Gatland's first match at the Millennium Stadium in charge of Wales – he had enjoyed victory there before with Ireland in 2001. In their nine years playing at the ground, Wales had always changed in the room that stood to the right at the top of the stairs as the players entered the stadium. Gatland turned the visiting changing-room into the home one, which meant swapping the dugouts where the replacements and ancillary management staff sat, as well as exchanging the hospitality boxes where the two coaching teams watched matches from. 'In the old dressing-room, some of the players were behind you when you were addressing them,' said Gatland. 'You can hear and see everyone in the room we are using now. It was not a move I imposed on the players. I consulted them, and they were comfortable with the switch.' Gatland was not worried about the reputation the room had for being a curse to those who used it: the first 12 football sides who changed there in the days when Cardiff hosted major matches while Wembley was being redeveloped all lost, and a feng shui expert had been hired to hustle away supposed evil spirits. It had hardly been unkind to Gatland seven years before when Ireland defeated Wales 36–6. 'I do not know anything about curses,' he said. 'The away room simply has a better ambience about it, and no one should get emotionally attached to changing-rooms. What do four walls do for a team's performance? They will now be known as rooms one and two instead of home and away.'

New broom, new room. But it was the same story as

at Twickenham, with Scotland kicking an early penalty after the break to draw within a point of Wales. The Scots were offering no threat with the ball in hand, but Wales's discipline was less impressive than it had been at Twickenham. The essential difference between the two sides was Wales's ability to create and react. When Phillips's pass to Hook inside Scotland's 25 went behind the outside-half, it seemed as if yet another move would break down through an unforced error, but the prop Duncan Jones was on hand to pick up the ball with his back to the line 20 yards out. Tight forwards regularly fan out across the line in the modern game and mostly charge into a tackler, but instead of turning, sticking his head down and running, Jones spotted Hook looping around him and timed his pass to perfection. Hook continued his outside arc and, with two Scottish front-row forwards ahead of him, had the pace to make the line. One more score and the game was won, but within thirteen minutes Hook had been substituted after committing a series of errors, although the spectators were perplexed when they realised it was Hook who was coming off for Stephen Jones.

Wales's lead had been eroded to two points by the time Hook went off in the fifty-ninth minute, and the two penalties kicked by Paterson both followed mistakes made by the Wales outside-half. After receiving quick ruck ball just inside Scotland's half, he had ignored two players on the wide outside and was turned over. Southwell counter-attacked, Ian Evans was penalised for going off his feet at the breakdown and Paterson made no mistake from 30 yards. Three minutes later, Hook had again taken on defenders near halfway rather than kicking for position, and he was fortunate that the ball was seized by Martyn Williams when it went loose. The flanker's pass was intercepted by the Scotland scrum-half Mike Blair, who kicked it back into Welsh territory. Hook picked it up but was again turned over. A free-kick and a penalty to Scotland later, and the score was 17–15. Gatland immediately brought on Stephen Jones and Peel for Hook and Phillips.

'I took off James because he wasted a four-man overlap, got turned over and put us under pressure,' said Gatland. 'He is still developing as a player, and there are areas he needs to improve in. Stephen and Dwayne are two experienced players who were both part of the 2005 Grand Slam team. We were taking a long time to put away a team that was not offering an attacking threat. We were the only ones trying to play rugby, and when you have players who can make an impact from the bench, you have to use them. We were dominating the game in terms of territory, but we were keeping Scotland in it through our indiscipline. I felt we needed to utilise the experience we had in the final 20 minutes. Stephen took us to the line well, but we are still a few levels from where we need to be, and no team in the Six Nations will be working harder than we are.'

Jones kicked a penalty to take Wales to 20–15, effectively a two-score lead with Scotland not threatening in attack, but it took a moment of brilliance from Shane Williams, allied with a hint of controversy, to put the match beyond the Scots. Little appeared to be on when the wing appeared at outside-centre going left, but he weaved inside and outside on a forty-yard run, accelerating between the two Scottish centres, before hugging the left-hand touchline and diving through Nikki Walker's tackle to score in the corner. The New Zealand referee Bryce Lawrence called on the video official Carlo Damasco to adjudicate on whether

Williams had put a foot in touch before touching the ball down one-handed in a remarkable act of contortion. The initial replays suggested a fair score, which is how Damasco ruled, but one camera angle raised the strong suspicion that the wing's trailing left foot had scraped the whitewash. Frank Hadden, whose side had conceded a try to Jonny Wilkinson at Twickenham the year before on the ruling of a video referee even though the outside-half had clearly been pushed into touch, railed against the decision, but acknowledged that, despite the closeness of the score at the time, his side could not use the incident as an excuse, because they had been outplayed.

Jones kicked a late penalty to give Wales their biggest victory over Scotland in Cardiff for 14 years, and 30 was their highest tally in the fixture at home since 1972, not that the statistics impressed Gatland. Wales had spent two-thirds of the match in Scotland's half; they had completed 131 passes to 41, made 11 line breaks while Scotland could not manage any and won the ball in their opponents' 25 on 26 occasions compared with 15, with most of Scotland's tally coming in the final few minutes as they laid siege to the Wales line only to find an unbreachable wall in front of them. It was as if everyone in a Wales jersey was anticipating the reaction of Shaun Edwards if they conceded a try, and as they repulsed one thrust after another the crowd roared its support, the noise growing louder with each failed foray. It was the moment Edwards knew he had arrived.

'The crowd was challenging the players not to concede a try, and that was great to hear,' he said. 'I think the spectators came to appreciate that defence can be exciting. We had the game won by then, but the players realised the importance of keeping their line intact. The Scots were hammering away, but we held them out, and that really pleased me. I had tried to get across to the Welsh public that defence was important. We need to have pride in our defence, and to hear the crowd singing "Wales, Wales" when were defending our line was gratifying. They were as excited about us stopping tries as they were when we were scoring them. I found that hugely rewarding. What also pleased me was that we handled the tag of being made the favourites, even if there was a moment in the game when I wondered how we were only two points in front, because we had been the better team by far. We ran away with it at the end, and I think that people are starting to understand what I have long believed: it is a 22-man game, and the impact from the bench was very important for us. It is often the case that the player who comes on as a replacement has a bigger impact on the game than the guy who starts.'

Gatland said that he would again change a winning team when Italy visited the Millennium Stadium in the next round. He had substituted his captain, Ryan Jones, on the hour, while the prop Gethin Jenkins had come on 13 minutes into the second half. Just as he had singled out Popham for censure after Twickenham, this time he pointed a finger at the tight-head prop Adam Jones, even though the Osprey had made more tackles than any other Wales player. 'The first penalty they kicked was very disappointing,' he said. 'It came from their lineout, and we had talked beforehand about not getting into the jumper too early. I will be speaking to Adam Jones. That sort of error can cost you a game. We will be bringing in players for Italy, and there may perhaps be a change at half-back. We have to be more ruthless when it comes to putting teams away. We conceded too many penalties in the first half and gave away some stupid penalties. Discipline has to improve.'

The players who had to perform the ritual of speaking to the media on their way out of the stadium to the post-match function all downplayed the victory, highlighting the mistakes that had been made rather than focusing on what was ultimately a comprehensive victory. Such interviews, if they can be called that, with reporters crowded in a small area and jostling for position, often only hearing snatches of the words that are spoken, are rarely illuminating. Players are usually briefed about what and what not to say before they make their descent, but it was clear, following Twickenham, that a pattern was emerging. They knew they would be judged on their errors as much, if not more so, depending on the nature of a mistake, as their positive contributions. 'We have to develop our game and become more efficient,' said Stephen Jones. 'We have to review how we are starting matches. There is no margin for error, because this is the most competitive Welsh squad I can remember. You are judged by what you do in training as much as how you play in a match.'

Jones had remained on the bench at Twickenham, but the way he had made an immediate impact from the bench against Scotland ensured that the Welsh outside-half debate would be reignited. Whereas a year before, Gareth Jenkins had been pilloried in the media for preferring Jones in the position to Hook, Gatland was to escape with scarcely a breath of criticism. Opening with two victories fortified his position, but he was also fertilising a growing realism that success was about more than who played in a certain position. Whereas before the argument was about Jones or Hook, Gatland pointed to the fact that it was now about

Jones and Hook. Both undid Scotland, Hook by creating and scoring Wales's opening tries and providing a threat off his side's own possession, when defences were at their most organised, and Jones by adding leadership and direction. What Hook started, Jones finished off. Wales were encouraging Hook to follow Jones's example and become more vocal and demonstrative. The management had felt that one of the problems at Twickenham had been that the initial outside-half/centre combination of Hook, Henson and Sonny Parker was made up of three largely silent types while Jones and Shanklin offered more in terms of communication.

There was no one, though, to rival Shane Williams on the left wing. His second try might have been disputed by the Scots, but its execution was marking out Wales from the other teams in the championship, even France. Williams was not content to stay on his wing, but roamed around looking for the ball. 'I have been given a licence by the coaches,' he said, 'although they have reminded me not to expect the ball in my hands all the time!' Wales had taken flight, and no one was soaring higher than the Osprey.

4

....

RUDDOCKLESS

The paths of glory lead but to the grave.

Thomas Gray

14 FEBRUARY 2006. IT IS THE MIDDLE OF THE AFTER-
noon and the Wales head coach Mike Ruddock is
sitting in his office in the Barn at the Vale of Glamorgan
Hotel wrestling with a conundrum. Gavin Henson is
available for selection again after serving a 72-day ban
for striking an opponent during a Heineken Cup match
between the Ospreys and Leicester. The return of the
centre, who had played a major role in the Grand Slam
success the previous year, should not be a cause for
head-scratching. But it is not as simple as that. Wales,
as was the case after their other two successful seasons
in the preceding eighteen years, 1988 and 1994, are in
meltdown. Henson is not a popular figure in the squad

after publishing his revelatory autobiography at the end of 2005. As Ruddock ponders, fresh in his mind will be the events of a week before, which, even by the standards of Welsh rugby, whose dictionary defines the word drama as a crisis, were extraordinary.

The media had gathered in the headquarters of Glamorgan County Cricket Club in Cardiff for the announcement of the Wales team to face Scotland at the Millennium Stadium that Saturday. Wales had lost heavily to England at Twickenham the previous weekend, ending a run of six successive victories in the Six Nations, and there was a sizeable turnout with a larger number of reporters from London-based newspapers than normal. There had been suggestions since the autumn, culminating in a newspaper article in November, that there was increasing discontent in the Wales squad, with some senior players privately questioning Ruddock's methods, but the public line was that everything was harmonious. The events at Sophia Gardens shattered that illusion, and a week later Ruddock was the former Wales head coach.

The protocol for the team announcement was that Ruddock and his captain, Gareth Thomas, would sit at the top table answering questions for 15 minutes before players were made available for interview in an adjoining room, divided into separate groups for morning newspapers, evenings, Sundays and broadcasters. Thomas, who had been appointed captain by Ruddock in 2004, to the surprise of many, came into the room and started walking towards the top table. Suddenly, he turned around and walked back out. He did not return, and Ruddock later came in alone to go through the team and answer questions. The media then left for the room next door and sat at their respective tables, waiting for the players to arrive. Waiting and waiting. Apart from one journalist who had been interviewing the wing Mark Jones while the team announcement was being made, no one knew what was going on. Ruddock came in to sit at the various tables individually, something he usually did after the players had fulfilled their duties, and shrugged when asked where the players were. It was some forty minutes before they trooped in with no explanation given for their very late arrival, although speculation started that Thomas had objected to the presence of one reporter in the room and had performed his abrupt about-turn when he saw him.

The conjecture quickly turned to fact. The reporter in question was Graham Thomas, the presenter of BBC Wales's rugby magazine programme *Scrum V.* Thomas had ghosted Henson's autobiography, some of the details in which, coupled with Henson's contention at his book launch that his teammates had no problems with what he had written, had so upset Gareth Thomas the previous December that he had called a meeting of the players and asked Henson to explain himself. Graham Thomas had then written an opinion column in the England–Wales match programme at Twickenham in which he championed the cause of free speech and lauded Henson for his candour, comparing him favourably to the cliché-riddled, politically correct and spin-doctor-approved utterances customarily given by players in the professional era.

Graham Thomas had written:

> Honest opinion should be encouraged. Most players will continue to hide behind the bland sound bite, the opinionless opinion. If there are a few who dare to be different, then supporters, sponsors and

especially the media, should all be extremely grateful. It is difficult to see why Henson, a professional player in his early 20s who comes from a working-class background, should feel constrained by a set of principles that have a distinct whiff of class, privilege and public schools.

Gareth Thomas read the article and took umbrage with it, feeling that a wound he believed had been stitched and healed had been gratuitously reopened. At his instigation, a complaint was made to BBC Wales by the Wales team manager Alan Phillips, and it was agreed that Graham Thomas would not attend the team announcement for the Scotland match. The problem was that no one had told Graham Thomas, and when Gareth Thomas saw him, he presumed the reporter had wilfully disregarded an instruction.

After leaving the room where the team announcement was to be made, Gareth Thomas went back to the restaurant at Sophia Gardens where the rest of the players, Mark Jones excepted, were gathered. He told them what had happened and said he did not want any of them to conduct media interviews until Graham Thomas had left the building. Ruddock came into the room and asked Gareth Thomas to come back out with him for the team announcement. Thomas refused. Ruddock turned to Michael Owen, the vice-captain and a player Ruddock had coached at Newport Gwent Dragons, and asked him if he would join him. Owen said he was sticking with Thomas, leaving the head coach to go into the media room alone. Only after Graham Thomas had left the building, 40 minutes later, did the players emerge.

Thomas said in his autobiography, *Alfie!*, that it was the squad, not just he, who had an issue with the programme article:

> Alan Phillips and I met Nigel Walker [BBC Wales's head of sport] to register our concerns. Nigel agreed to our request not to deal with Graham Thomas for the week of the Scotland game. It was a stand that the team felt we had to make, and it was very much a decision taken by the whole squad, not just me . . . It emerged that Graham Thomas had not had the message about our temporary refusal to deal with him and, to be fair to him, he was not there in an act of defiance. Understandably, he was not prepared to go anywhere. As far as I was concerned, that was it. There was no way I was going to speak to the media while he remained in attendance. Simon Rimmer [the Wales squad's communications manager] and Mike were of the view that we should just go in and get the media conference over with, but I was having none of it. The principle was no different to that of a picket line – you stand together with your colleagues and don't cross it just because the boss asks you to.

The following day, the squad apologised to Ruddock and to the media, but a line had been crossed: the players had followed their captain, not their head coach. There had, for months, been conjecture, prompted by in-house whispers, that all was not well between Ruddock and some of his players, and an act of public defiance was confirmation enough for most. The Welsh Rugby Union did not issue a public condemnation of the players' stand but instead broke off contract negotiations with the head coach. Ruddock had been appointed in the summer of 2004 on a two-year deal. The WRU said after the Grand Slam success that it would be negotiating an extension with Ruddock to take him through to the 2007 World Cup, and he shook hands on a deal towards the end of 2005, although he wanted to sort out a couple of clauses concerning disciplinary and grievance procedures before signing it; he was particularly concerned that one of his assistants, Scott Johnson, had not signed his contract and therefore had no job description or chain of command. A meeting was arranged with Ruddock's solicitor, Tim Jones, the father of the second row Alun Wyn Jones, who was to be a member of the 2008 Grand Slam squad, but the WRU did not bring a copy of the contract with them and nothing was resolved. The contract issue became a fixation for the media before the start of the 2006 Six Nations, but there were assurances from both Ruddock and the union that it would be resolved quickly. It wasn't, and in the week of the Scotland game the WRU withdrew it from the table and said that negotiations would have to start again from the beginning.

Wales defeated Scotland 28–18, with Gareth Thomas scoring two tries, but Ruddock had already decided that he would not seek a renewal of his contract. He intended to see out the remaining four months of his deal, and on the morning of St Valentine's Day he let the WRU know. The union had no option but to accept, and as Ruddock returned to his office at the Vale of Glamorgan Hotel his focus was on planning for the trip to face Ireland in Dublin the following week with the Henson dilemma at the top of his considerations, not that the reaction of other players was a particular concern to him any more. News started leaking out: the *Western Mail*, the Cardiff-based morning newspaper, contacted Ruddock, and he confirmed that he would be standing down at the end of the season. The union had not set a time for a public announcement, but when the *Western Mail*'s interest was discovered, a media conference was hurriedly arranged for 9 p.m. in a hospitality box at the Millennium Stadium.

When the WRU chief executive Steve Lewis announced at the conference that Mike Ruddock had resigned, it was not a surprise. The grapevine had hummed in the three hours between the notice of the 9 p.m. meeting and its start. What was unexpected was Lewis's statement that Ruddock had stood down with immediate effect. The media conference was more notable for what was not said than for what was revealed. Calls made to some board directors in the early evening led to moments of silence when they were asked why Ruddock was going. They had not been told. The decision was made by the WRU's executive committee and presented as a fait accompli to the directors via the telephone. It was to be argued in the coming months that it had been an unconstitutional act and that a board meeting should have been arranged for a vote to be taken, but Ruddock had given notice that he would be not be seeking an extension of his deal.

The question was why he had not been allowed to work out his contract and, on top of that, who had made that call. A crib sheet left by one of the members of the top table, based on anticipated questions and suggested answers, included the following: 'Why is Mike Ruddock staying in charge for the next three matches rather than going immediately?' The recommended answer was: 'Mike Ruddock, Scott Johnson [the assistant coach] and Clive Griffiths [the defence coach] have been in place as a management team for the last two years. They are still in place and will be for the duration of the championship, so the Wales team is in a state of stability.' This crib sheet indicated just how late the decision had been not to allow Ruddock to stay on for the rest of the season.

Ostensibly, Ruddock's departure was for family reasons, which prompted the question why it had only been a few weeks before that the WRU had said he was close to signing a new contract. There was speculation that a delegation of senior players had met Steve Lewis the previous week to express their growing disenchantment with Ruddock. Lewis said in an interview with BBC Radio Wales, 'I received no documentation from any player regarding dissatisfaction with Mike Ruddock, and I've not had any meetings with any players. I am not aware of any unease in the camp about Mike's coaching. If players don't talk to me, they don't talk to other WRU leaders.'

In his autobiography, Thomas said that he and three other senior players, Martyn Williams, Stephen Jones and Brent Cockbain, had met with Lewis during the week of the Scotland game:

> The main purpose of the meeting was to clarify an insurance issue. It had been a concern to some of the boys after Gareth Cooper had gone off with a shoulder injury at Twickenham. The aim was to find out what the extent of our cover was from the WRU. I made it clear that unless we were covered for the worst type of injury imaginable, then we would consider withdrawing our services . . . Our

fears were allayed, so the matter never went any further. A few more run-of-the-mill issues were discussed and then I moved on to the subject of Mike Ruddock. I told Steve of my concerns that Mike wasn't taking enough responsibility in the running of the team, considering that he was the head coach. Immediately, Steve tried to cut me off, but I had enough time to get a little further, saying that we all wanted Mike to be the one to take us forward. That wasn't happening at present, I continued. Steve did manage to get a word in, though he was quite abrupt in his response. He told us that if we had any issues, they would have to be between us and Mike. As far as the union was concerned, the coach would have their full backing.

Martyn Williams had a slightly different take on the talks with Lewis in his autobiography, *The Magnificent Seven*, which was published the month before the start of the 2008 Six Nations:

> We'd asked for the meeting as a squad to discuss insurance cover, but because things had not gone so well, Steve asked a few questions and just sort of said: 'What's going on boys?' If you believe some of the things you have read, this is where we said Ruddock had to go. That simply was not the case. We didn't say we wanted him out or that we thought he should go. What we did say was that we felt that perhaps we'd slipped back into old ways and gone back a few notches. Steve asked us the question and

we were being honest. We also made it known that, whatever happened, from the players' point of view we couldn't lose Scott Johnson. We had lost Steve Hansen and Andrew Hore and we just said whatever you do you've got to try and keep Johnno because we felt that if we were going to keep on developing, we needed him there. We owed him so much and we were adamant that the WRU had to do everything in their power to try and keep hold of him. A lot has been made of the meeting, but there was no personal attack on Mike and it was never a case of us saying we wanted to get rid of him. It was just purely that we felt we had let a lot of things slip.

The WRU chairman David Pickering sat alongside Lewis at the media conference, along with Scott Johnson, who had been appointed caretaker coach for the rest of the Six Nations. Lewis said he had met with Ruddock that morning, adding, 'Mike told me that he would not be seeking an extension of his contract for personal and family reasons, even though we had reached agreement on its terms. We both agreed that it would have been in his and the team's best interests if he stood down immediately. This has come as a shock.' Asked whether he had wanted Ruddock to stay, Pickering replied, 'That is hypothetical. We were put in a position of crisis today, but we have dealt with it. We have formulated a strategy, and we are implementing it. Mike is a wonderful coach and a true gentleman.'

The former Wales captain Eddie Butler, the rugby correspondent with *The Observer* and a BBC pundit, asked Johnson to pay tribute to Ruddock. 'He's a good coach,' was the reply. Butler observed that it did not amount to a ringing endorsement of Johnson's erstwhile head coach. 'What do you want me to say?' was the retort. 'Mike is a great coach. He's a wonderful human being. Is that better?' Tensions were running high. The official line had not been bought. It promised to be the start of a very long and trying few weeks.

Little more than 12 hours later, Johnson and Michael Owen fronted a media conference at the Barn in the Vale of Glamorgan complex (Gareth Thomas was in France, training with his club, Toulouse) that was supposed to look ahead to the Ireland match, but the reporters present were more interested in looking back. Johnson indicated that he would be returning to his native Australia in the summer, having been offered a job on the Wallabies' management team, adding that he had been shocked by Ruddock's departure and that he had had no designs on taking over the head coach's job on a permanent basis. Ruddock had gone to ground, although he issued a statement clarifying one issue: when he had told the WRU that he would not be seeking a renewal of his contract, the agreement had been that he would continue in position until the end of the season. 'I received a request from my employers on Tuesday night [14 February] to stand down with immediate effect. I respected their wishes and agreed to leave my post immediately.' The call came shortly before the start of the announcement of his departure the previous night. Ruddock was put on gardening leave.

Pickering's hope that the crisis had been managed disappeared under a wave of anger. The WRU's paid executive came under pressure from the amateur, elected board directors who had not been privy to events as they had unfolded on 14 February. Ruddock's request to meet the board on the following Tuesday was agreed as a rising tide of opinion held player power to blame for the coach's departure. Butler, in his newspaper column, pointed the finger at Johnson, writing that when Ruddock took over from Steve Hansen he

> agreed to work with the coaching staff – Johnson and Andrew Hore [conditioning] – who had been left behind by Hansen, bringing in just Clive Griffiths, his defence coach at the Dragons. This was where the troubles began. Johnson was soon sniping at Griffiths. Ruddock was aware of the undercurrent and had to ward off Johnson. In the autumn [of 2005], the sniping grew worse. Johnson complained to the players that Ruddock was delegating too much to him, while the head coach spent too much time out shopping with his wife. Out of the camp came the story that Ruddock was known as 'The Bus' because he was not a coach . . . Ruddock found himself increasingly at odds with some of the very performers he had empowered as part of his credo of giving responsibility to his performers. And the source of the discontent was not hard to find. He had to reprimand Johnson for missing coaching meetings. On three occasions he had to confront him on the issue of undermining him. The trouble for Ruddock was the bond between Johnson and the players. Johnson never scotched the rumour that he might up and leave at any moment. The players grew ever more determined to have him stay.

It was an instant analysis that has stood the test of time.

Events spiralled out of control for the WRU as conspiracy theories abounded. There was an angry reaction from the Welsh public. Johnson's popularity within the squad might have forced the union's hand, but Ruddock's stock within the wider rugby community was high. The WRU was pushed on to the defensive, and although a meeting of the board of directors agreed that the executive had acted within its rights by telling Ruddock to go immediately, it did not amount to an endorsement of the action, no matter how much the union tried to spin it that way. Clubs were threatening to call an emergency general meeting and table a vote of no confidence in the board. The union responded by hosting a series of what were called red zone meetings: senior officials visited each of the nine districts that made up the WRU to explain the circumstances that had led to Ruddock going. Some of the meetings became heated, especially those where questioners came well armed. At one gathering, three questions were asked that had been drawn up with the help of Ruddock, who had supplied the answers as he knew them to be true. The WRU's responses did not tally with them, and the lack of clarity remained. The subject was off limits to the national squad when it came to media interviews, but the events were clearly preying on their mind, because they lost heavily in Dublin before drawing with Italy at the Millennium Stadium and finishing with a narrow defeat to France in Cardiff, just avoiding the wooden spoon.

Gareth Thomas was no longer the captain. On the Sunday following Ruddock's departure, he had agreed to be interviewed on *Scrum V*. Under questioning from Butler and another former Wales captain, Jonathan Davies, the atmosphere grew steadily heated. The message Thomas tried to get across at every opportunity was that the players had not put pressure on the WRU to get rid of Ruddock. 'I went to see Steve Lewis because we had issues we wanted to raise, and Mike knew we went to see the chief executive,' he said on the programme. 'What we need to remember here is that it wasn't just Mike who won the Grand Slam. We actually laced our boots up and other coaches came in and helped. As captain, I think we should let the credit spread everywhere, and I think Mike would agree.' Thomas felt that he had been stitched up, and it was perhaps a sign of how the WRU was losing the public-relations battle that he was allowed to go on the programme while the air was still thick with emotion. When he returned home to watch his interview, which had been pre-recorded, he collapsed and was taken to hospital. He had suffered a burst blood vessel in his neck, which caused a mini-stroke. 'I thought I was dying,' he said. He was ruled out of action for the rest of the season, and, for a while, there was concern that he would not play again.

Pickering wrote to BBC Wales to complain about the interview, claiming that a protocol agreed beforehand had been ignored, something the BBC denied. The following Friday, Steve Lewis was sitting in the stand at Athlone watching the Under-21 international between Ireland and Wales. It was televised on the BBC, and the director cut to a shot of the WRU's chief executive. Someone called Lewis to tell him that he had appeared on screen. He then left his seat and went down to pitch level to complain to the programme's floor manager. A WRU communications official soon appeared in the outside broadcast truck to complain about intrusion. When the fuss died down, Butler was removed from *Scrum V*, along with Graham Thomas.

In retrospect, the likeliest conclusion is that the Ruddock affair was an unfortunate coming together of events rather than a conspiracy. It was like a snowball that, as it rolled, gathered momentum and became so large that no one could stop it, and it duly had a flattening effect. There was no great desire among the players for Ruddock to go, merely a fear towards the end that if he stayed, Johnson would return to Australia, or join Leicester, a club with which he had been linked. Johnson had been with the Wales squad since the end of 2001, brought in first by Graham Henry and then staying on under Steve Hansen. He had become the players' guru.

Ruddock took over a settled squad that was building on the strong showing at the 2003 World Cup. He changed little and was happy to delegate. That was perhaps his undoing, and while it worked with Wales winning the Grand Slam in 2005, it also worked against him, because he remained an outsider.

It was an episode that saw nobody win: Ruddock lost his job, Johnson returned to Australia one month after the end of the Six Nations and Griffiths did not have his contract renewed. Steve Lewis left the WRU after the clubs called an extraordinary general meeting and voted to restore the position of group chief executive. Roger Lewis was appointed and quickly set about reorganising the departments under him. Michael Owen took over the captaincy after Gareth Thomas's illness, but he lost his place when Gareth Jenkins took over the following May. He went to the World Cup but did not feature in Gatland's Six Nations campaign. And after winning five out of five in 2005, Wales were triumphant in only two of the next ten Six Nations matches.

Ruddock has maintained a dignified silence since that February night in 2006. He took a year out of professional rugby, working for a recruitment agency and helping out at Mumbles Rugby Club. He became Worcester's head coach in the summer of 2007 and immediately appointed Clive Griffiths, who after leaving Wales had become Doncaster's director of rugby, as his defence coach. Speaking after Wales had won the 2008 Grand Slam, Ruddock said he hoped a line would now be drawn under the events that led up to his leaving a job he had wanted for so long after less than two years in the position.

'The main reason I said nothing was that I did not want to undermine Welsh rugby,' he said. 'Everything was in turmoil, and there was nothing to be gained in speaking out. It would only have made matters worse. Things are on a much more even keel now, and I am absolutely delighted at the immediate impact Warren Gatland has made. I know him from our days in Ireland a decade ago when he was initially in charge of Connacht and I was coaching Leinster. I wrote him a letter of congratulation when he arrived in Wales, and he sent me a warm response. I think now, at long last, the game in Wales can look forward. Warren has certainly absorbed the lessons of the last two years. He has insisted on his own management team, and, from the first minute of his time in the job, he has left no one in doubt as to who is in charge. It is a slightly different management style from the one I remember him adopting in Ireland, but it is a reflection of what he inherited. That shows how shrewd he is, and I am confident that Wales can move on from here and manage success. The core of his side was around in 2005, and there has never been any doubt about the quality of the players in the Wales squad. I have long wanted to draw a line over what happened two years ago, and maybe now, at last, I can. Perhaps the pain I felt, and there was a lot of it, will have been worth it if it means that Wales will be a force again.'

He still saw no merit in answering claims about the affair made subsequently in books and articles. 'Things happened, and I did feel isolated, particularly at the end, but there was nothing to be gained in pointing fingers at individuals at the time. I wanted to see out my contract, but the WRU had a late change of mind after agreeing to it initially. It hurt hugely at the time, and if I had my chance again, I would do things differently. I did not apply for the Wales post in 2004: the WRU approached me, and when you are offered the job of coaching your country, it is very difficult to turn it down. I do not regret not insisting on my own coaching team because I liked the way Wales had played during the World Cup, the WRU wanted minimum disruption and I was used to coming in to fairly settled environments and working with coaches I had never teamed up with before, notably with Wales A, Ireland A and Ireland, where I worked with Brian Ashton and Warren Gatland for a short time. I only brought in Clive Griffiths, and that was because defence was an area we needed to improve in. And we did. It was a major factor behind the Grand Slam success. Clive is a coach out of the very top drawer, and it was heartening to hear Shaun Edwards say after Wales had beaten France to win the Grand Slam that he regarded Clive as one of his mentors and that he was still in regular contact with him. What I did not appreciate was the extent of the resentment some on my management team felt towards Clive after his time with Wales between 2001 and 2003. He had been moved on to Newport Gwent Dragons after the World Cup because the Welsh management group at that time did not want to work with him. I'm not sure why Clive and some of the other members of the coaching team had fallen out previously, but even though Clive and I tried hard to make things work, there was just too much of a divide.

'I think Wales have a big future under Warren. He has a squad full of quality, and virtually all of the players will be around for the next World Cup. What would create difficulty is if it breaks up from within because the coaches are not pulling together, as happened in 2005. But I cannot see that occurring. Warren and Shaun go back a long time, and Robert Howley was with them at Wasps, and there is a loyalty to one another. They have learned from what has happened in the last two years. They have brought closure to a sad episode in our game. I have not been comfortable talking about what happened in 2006, but I could never seem to get away from it. Perhaps we can now bury that unfortunate period in the past.

'Would I have done anything differently? I do not regret taking the job, and no one can expunge the 2005 Grand Slam from the records, but perhaps it would have been better if I had had my own coaching team, given that I had underestimated the ill-feeling in the coaching group that my bringing back Clive, who had been moved on by my predecessor, Steve Hansen, after the World Cup, provoked, and to this day I do not understand why there was such ill-feeling towards him. I don't regret not being stricter or more of a disciplinarian, as I felt that to get the best out of the players they needed to play and train in a more relaxed manner with a greater emphasis on being able to express themselves rather than being directed by an iron fist and being heavily programmed each step of the way; getting away from the "Jail of Glamorgan mentality", if you like. To some it seemed to be undermining what Steve Hansen had developed, but I never meant it to be interpreted that way; otherwise, I felt on taking over that not a lot needed tinkering with: Scott Johnson was already doing a great job on the attack, Clive improved the defence and I worked on the set-pieces. It all seemed pretty simple! There was no point in ripping everything up; that would have been a nonsense. We played some terrific rugby in 2005, and we could have gone on from that. Looking back, I came into a settled management environment and brought in only Clive, a man whose coaching ability I rate very highly. For some reason, Clive's arrival split the management team, and because of my friendship with Clive I think some always saw me as an outsider; ultimately, you are not going to get anywhere if you are divided. The weight of trying to keep everything and everyone together became a major difficulty, and because of that the players did not see the best of me in 2006. I have always enjoyed coaching; however, the position of national coach became the least enjoyable coaching role I have ever experienced because of the divide in the coaching group and the management difficulties they presented.'

Ruddock's track record as a coach speaks for itself. He enjoyed success at Cross Keys, Swansea and Leinster before returning to Ebbw Vale and then Newport Gwent Dragons. He was not short of offers on leaving Wales but chose to take a year out before taking his first plunge into the Guinness Premiership. 'I am loving it at Worcester,' he said. 'The Premiership is even harder than I anticipated it would be, and we struggled for results early on. There is a real intensity and quality to the competition and matches attract big crowds. There are a number of people who I worked with that I have not seen since I left my job with Wales, and that part of my life is over. People should now be talking about the 2008 Grand Slam and the great times that lie ahead for the Welsh game; and we can look forward with confidence because what happened in 2005 has finally been addressed and dealt with.'

The pity for Ruddock's successor, Gareth Jenkins, is that it had been anything but settled when he took the job in May 2006, 16 months before the start of the World Cup. If Ruddock had not been the victim of player power, if that is interpreted as players going to the WRU and demanding that the coach be dismissed and getting their way, they achieved a strength in unity that eventually undermined Jenkins, and the fact that the WRU had not backed Ruddock when his position as head coach demanded its support was indicative of the dismissive way the union had treated the job over the years, even though it was the most important one in the Welsh game. Jenkins left a legacy for Gatland, capping James Hook before he had made an appearance for the Ospreys and bringing on the emerging second rows Alun Wyn Jones and Ian Evans. He appointed his own coaching team, but they were largely inexperienced, and it was not long before the whispering campaigns that had blown up in 2005 started again. Like Ruddock, he had long coveted the job and had been denied it in the past at the moment he had thought it was his, but his twenty matches in charge yielded only six victories and a draw, and critics were calling for his head long before Wales left for the World Cup.

Jenkins's sacking meant he became the sixth successive Welsh national coach, as in someone who was born in Wales, to depart ahead of schedule. Wales had had a number of foreign coaches in that time, and players seemed to respond better to an outsider who was not from a club or an area in Wales and whose claim to have no favourites would be universally accepted. Hansen, a former policeman, was a disciplinarian who involved himself in every aspect of squad life. In his autobiography, *Staying Strong*, Robin McBryde, the Wales forwards coach under Jenkins who retained his job when Gatland arrived, wrote:

> Steve places great importance on values, and I still remember the six he stressed. Respect, unity, belief, honesty, enjoyment and resilience formed the basis of his gospel. I remember one incident when we were preparing for an international match and had been asked to stay together at the Vale of Glamorgan Hotel for the preceding week. One of our wingers decided he would spend a night at home in the middle of the week and return the following morning. Unfortunately for him, when he returned at breakfast time Steve happened to be in the foyer and asked where he had been. The reply was that he had been out to his car to get a CD. Steve could not see him carrying it and asked where it was. The winger said he couldn't find it. 'You haven't been home, then?' asked Steve. No was the answer. Steve repeated the question twice more and got the same reply. The player went to his room, and Steve went to the car park. It was a cold morning, and the frost was plainly to be seen on the cars which had been parked overnight. Steve noticed there was no frost on the winger's car and that the bonnet and exhaust pipe were warm. Steve went up to the miscreant's room and, despite being given three further opportunities

to admit that he had been home, continued to deny that he had left the Vale. He had to go home fairly soon afterwards because Steve threw him out of the squad. It seems that his reasons for doing so were that he had been lied to, not because the player concerned had left the hotel.

There was a sad inevitability about Jenkins's end. He fell out with a section of the media and before the start of the World Cup had refused to answer questions at media conferences from representatives of one newspaper. The senior players' committee became increasingly influential, with one report claiming that they had insisted that a training session be cancelled. 'Gareth Jenkins made mistakes and allowed discipline in the squad to slip,' said the former Wales captain Ieuan Evans, who had played under Jenkins at Llanelli and for Wales in the early 1990s when the coach was an assistant in Alan Davies's regime, after the early World Cup exit. 'There is no way Gareth would have coached the players to play the way they did in the first half against Fiji. There is a culture of complacency: the players are having an undue influence, and when the new coach is appointed, it is an issue he must address. I am sorry that the WRU did not allow Gareth the dignity of returning home from France before making the announcement that he had been sacked. His appointment was a populist one, and you have to see the timing of his dismissal in the same light.'

The Ruddock affair had claimed a second victim. By denying there had been a problem, the WRU was unable to sort it out, and Jenkins, a passionate, committed and deeply knowledgeable coach, was scandalously hung out to dry on his own. In his book, McBryde recounts the events of the

Wales squad's final day in France:

The players looked on in disbelief when they were told Gareth was no longer in charge, not being able to take in the fact the decision had been taken so suddenly. Gareth, with great difficulty, addressed the squad briefly, and that was it. In no time we were on the team bus and on our way to the airport. It was one of the quietest journeys I had ever been on, with most of the party trying to get their heads around the events of the last two days.

We left Cardiff Wales Airport via a side exit in order to avoid the large media contingent that awaited our party and then arrived at the Vale of Glamorgan Hotel. I then witnessed one of the saddest sights I had ever experienced in rugby when Gareth Jenkins, in order to avoid the attention of the press, raised his hand to bid us all farewell and walked off the bus before it arrived at the hotel forecourt. That someone who had given so much to Welsh rugby was forced to depart in such an ignominious manner was hard to believe.

5

··

PUTTING THE BOOT IN

There is no such thing as great talent
without great will-power.

Honoré de Balzac

12 **FEBRUARY 2008. WARREN GATLAND HAS BEEN IN** charge of Wales for ten weeks having arrived with the force of a hurricane. The old order has been blown away: no one is occupying a comfort zone any more. He is sitting in a room at the Vale of Glamorgan Hotel, his face typically expressionless, ready to read out his side to face Italy at the Millennium Stadium the following week in yet another change of protocol.

The team would normally have been made public four days before the match, but Gatland wanted to maximise his preparation time. Just as he had changed a winning team after Twickenham, so Wales's biggest victory at home to Scotland for 14 years did not prompt him to say same again.

Italy were in their ninth season as a member of the Six Nations and had recorded only one away victory, at Scotland in 2007, but the nature of the championship had become so unpredictable that while Wales had beaten England in three of their previous four championship meetings, their record against Italy was less impressive. They had not beaten the Azzurri since the 2005 Grand Slam season and had won just two of the last five encounters, including a controversial defeat in Rome in 2007. It was a game that seemed to sum up the way fortune kept spitting in the face of Gareth Jenkins: Wales were trailing by three points in the final minute of stoppage time when they were awarded a kickable penalty. They preferred to go for the victory rather than the draw, and Gareth Thomas, who had taken over the captaincy when Stephen Jones left the field injured, asked the referee Chris White whether they had time to kick for touch and take a lineout. White replied that they did, and Wales kicked the ball out some six yards form Italy's line. As they went to prepare for the lineout, White was told by the fourth official that time was up and that he had to blow his whistle. He did so, first to the bemusement and then to the anger of the Wales players, some of whom surrounded him before shaking hands with their opposite numbers.

The laws of the game say that the referee is the sole judge of fact, but not on this occasion. Referees rarely comment on controversial incidents, but White issued a statement that ran, 'I would like to apologise for the misunderstanding as the game drew to a close on Saturday. I have apologised to the Wales management and the players for the misunderstanding. I would like to thank them for the good grace with which the apology was accepted.'

The Italy captain Alessandro Troncon, whose side had not profited unduly from refereeing decisions during their time in the Six Nations, was unsympathetic: 'Wales had ten seconds left to play when the penalty was awarded, but the referee was correct because the Welsh players spent too much time talking about what to do. Fortunately for us, the official correctly decided to blow his whistle.' Time was not on Jenkins's side.

Wales had had a plan that day to keep the ball in open play as often as possible. They did not want to kick to touch and give Italy the opportunity to catch the ball at a lineout and drive mauls. The problem was that they spent too much time in possession in their own half and kept getting turned over. Under Gatland, Wales refined their kicking game: in James Hook, Gavin Henson and Lee Byrne, they had players who could boot the ball a considerable distance, and their new defensive system demanded a quick chase to reduce the time the opponent who gathered the ball had to weigh up his options. Wales's tactics against Italy in the 2008 Six Nations were not markedly different from those of the year before. The difference lay in the execution and the unquestioning acceptance of them by the players.

The 2006 draw against Italy in Cardiff had effectively sounded the last post on the style that had taken Wales to the Grand Slam. It was a game based on movement, off-loading and pace. Wales were as threatening when they had the ball on their own line as they were when they were in the opposition's 25, but they had become predictable, as one-dimensional as a team that never moved the ball wider than the outside-half. They started to struggle at the breakdown and found themselves turned over in their own half. Having established a lead against Italy, they did not play for position and seek the score that would have closed the game out. Their game lacked pragmatism and had no boundaries.

When the former England and Lions coach Dick Best suggested immediately after the 2005 Grand Slam that the success would be a one-off because it was, in his words, built on a foundation of sand rather than a strong forward platform and that the lack of structure to Wales's game would become a weakness when opponents worked out ways of stopping them, his observation was lost in the euphoria of the moment and a stream of invective flowed his way, but time was to prove him correct. Wales were not evolving, and while in 2008 they rarely conceded in the final 20 minutes of matches, in 2006 they did not score once in the final quarter. The team, booed off the field less than a year after being feted as heroes, was ready for a change of direction. Gareth Jenkins talked about adopting a more pragmatic approach when he took over from Ruddock, who himself had recognised the need to mix things up more before his abrupt departure, but he failed to convince his players, who were still fixatedly committed to the keep-the-ball-in-hand-and-run-from-everywhere approach of Scott Johnson.

Wales had become mentally tougher in their two matches under Gatland, but his team to face Italy surprised the players and the media. He had warned there would be changes, but no one expected six new faces, or just seven Ospreys. Stephen Jones and Dwayne Peel came in at half-back, Mark Jones returned on the wing for Jamie Roberts and there was a new-look front row, with Gethin Jenkins,

Matthew Rees and Rhys Thomas all starting. It amounted to a considerably more experienced team than the one that had faced Scotland: with the exception of Rhys Thomas, who had won three caps compared with the forty-six of the player he replaced, Adam Jones, the players who came in had won more caps than those they had taken over from. Additionally, Stephen Jones, Peel and Jenkins had started every match in the 2005 Grand Slam season. After two victories, Wales were finding themselves being talked up: they were already one victory away from the Triple Crown and with England struggling, France pursuing a bizarre selection policy that saw players coming and going with performance no sort of barometer, and Ireland humming with the same mouldy mustiness that had cut short their World Cup campaign, it was no longer fanciful to tip Wales for the title.

Gatland said he had been surprised about one aspect of his players. 'Before I came over to Wales, I spoke to some people, and the consensus was that I would be working with a group who were lacking in basic skills,' he said. 'They are as good as Kiwis when it comes to handling and passing, and they are better in that respect than the Irish and English players I have worked with. What they have to learn is to play with intensity under pressure and be more accurate. We wasted opportunities against Scotland, and that is where we have to be more accurate. We have to keep reminding ourselves of small, critical moments that are important to us going forward. Skill levels may be high, but physically we have a lot of work to do over the next 18 months if we are to compete against the best teams in the world. At least we have a base we can win from.' He felt that the goldfish bowl that was Welsh rugby hindered players, because reactions to their performances were intemperate: they were either world beaters or rubbish. He was then asked why Hook had been dropped. 'James will be a fantastic player going forward,' he replied. 'He is very, very good in broken play: he has fantastic feet and makes brilliant little off-loads. Sensational is the only word for some of his skills. What we need with that free-spirited rugby is an element of control, something Stephen Jones brings. James has to learn to be a little more structured at times, more dominant in the game. I am not worried about his progress, and this gives him a bit of breathing space.'

Speaking to Sunday newspaper reporters later, he went into more detail about Hook, showing that his paramount concern was for the team, not for the individuals who made it up. The game in Wales had a reputation for being a haven for romantics, but Gatland only did hard-nosed realism, and, as he said in one of his first interviews, he would far rather win a game 3–0 than lose one 48–46. 'It is hard for top rugby players in Wales, because they are superstars in a cocoon,' he said. 'They are put on a pedestal, but they always have to remind themselves to keep their feet on the ground. People are talking about James Hook being a superstar. I would say to him, "Remember, you missed a kick against Fiji in the World Cup which cost us a quarter-final spot." We have to be level-headed. Players in Wales tend to get paid more than their English counterparts. We have to keep reminding them about working hard, harder than other countries. We have to be aware of what people are thinking about us and what they are saying about us.'

Gatland said that Mark Jones was brought back after missing one match because of the positive attitude he had shown in training following his demotion. 'I have worked hard on my defence,' said Jones. 'I was the only player in the backline against England not familiar with the blitz defence, and I had had less than two weeks adapting to it. I have been playing senior rugby for eight years and am used to a slide defence, and it has meant that I have had to do a lot of work on my own to get up to speed with the new system. It was bitterly disappointing to be left out after England, but the coaches said that training sessions would be taken into account when it came to selection, and they have been true to their word. As a professional sportsman, you have to deal with highs and lows. I have been laid up with serious injuries in my career, and I have always battled back. My view is that what does not kill you makes you stronger. I am not a sulker. Once Warren highlighted what I needed to do to get my place back, I went all out to put things right. He felt that at times against England my instinct was taking over in defence, and that is the area I have been concentrating on.'

Whereas the senior players' committee had had a strong influence in the previous regimes, equality was Gatland's policy. By changing winning sides and showing players that no one could take his place for granted, no one was under any illusions about who was in charge. 'The good thing about Warren and Shaun Edwards is that it does not matter how many caps you have won or how long you have been in the game, they will let you know immediately if you are doing something wrong or not pulling your weight,' said Martyn Williams, the side's most experienced player. 'In the past, we have often cruised through sessions because they went on for so long, but now there is no holding back, and each one is filmed for scrutiny afterwards. You are kept on the edge, and things sometimes spill over, with the competition for places so intense, but to me that is the sign of a good team. Some coaches will not pick up senior players when they make mistakes in training, but that is not the case with this regime. No exceptions are made, and that is good for the younger guys in the squad, because they know that everyone is being judged on how they perform, not on reputation. There are no half measures with this management team. Everything is black and white with Warren; there are no grey areas. He is firm but also relaxed; he is laid-back and does not shout and bawl. Every team in any sport will have a senior group, and how they are managed is very important. Give players an inch and we will take a mile. There is no chance of that happening with the guys in charge now. It reminds me of the time when Steve Hansen was around: you were always looking over your shoulder, because he involved himself in absolutely everything.'

Whereas the decision of Gareth Jenkins the year before to play Stephen Jones at outside-half rather than Hook had generated a tidal wave of criticism in the media that became distastefully personal, it was not an issue under Gatland, even though Hook had helped turn the match at Twickenham and had been involved in the opening two tries against Scotland. In the *Western Mail*, the former Wales captain Gwyn Jones wrote:

> I am an admirer of Hook's unquestionable skills, but I must admit that I am glad to see Stephen Jones in the number 10 shirt. He endured an unacceptable amount of criticism during last year's Six Nations and World Cup. Jones is nothing if not fully committed, and he has made the most of every morsel of talent

that he has got. Jones will never be able to do the things that Hook does on the field – he does not possess the youngster's guile and flair. However, he has the authority and the presence which come from experience. While Hook is learning his trade and honing his skills, it is vital that Jones remains a key part of the squad. I am sure that Hook will one day provide the leadership qualities that Jones brings, but for the time being at least, these are attributes he can learn from his rival for the much-vaunted outside-half jersey.

The selection of Jones was interpreted in many quarters as a tightening-up by Gatland, of a desire to play the game in Italy's half and not play into the hands of a side that had limited options behind the scrum. The Italians had opened with a 16–11 defeat to Ireland in Dublin, but the gap between the sides was wider than the scoreboard reflected. They came even closer in their second match, losing 23–19 at home to England, but, again, they never looked like winning the game. Nick Mallett, the former South Africa coach who had been in charge of the Springboks when they defeated Wales 96–13 in Pretoria in 1998, had taken over from Pierre Berbizier after the World Cup, but if there had been constant complaints in Wales after 2006 about the structure of the domestic game, Mallett's resources were far slimmer. There was no outside-half in Italy of international quality, and Mallett fielded a centre, Andrea Masi, in the position. He had no kicking game and struggled from the start, although he was to finish the championship strongly against Scotland.

Like Wales, Italy had been slow starters in their first two

matches, but they had a renowned set of scrummagers, and some observers were surprised when Gatland announced Rhys Thomas, who had struggled up front against South Africa the previous November, had taken the place of Adam Jones. It was less of a shock when Gatland's condemnation of Jones for conceding an early penalty – for taking Nathan Hines out in the air – that provided Scotland with their first points was taken into account. The head coach was angry because it was something he had worked on in training. He might have left out Jones anyway, with Wales's biggest two matches to come, but no one could be sure, and that was the environment he set out to create. He also had words of advice for the match referee, David Pearson. 'Italy got away with a lot in the tackle against England,' he said. 'They did not stay on their feet, and they should have been dealt with.' He had no real cause for concern: English referees had a reputation for being hard on defending players who tended not to stay on their feet at the breakdown, and Pearson was to penalise the Italians three times in the opening nine minutes for such indiscretions. When Wales went off their feet at a ruck two yards from the Italy line in the build-up to their opening try, they got away with it.

There was also a concern that Italy, knowing they would struggle in an open, fast game, would resort to foul play. Their flanker Mauro Bergamasco was banned for a month after the 2007 match between the sides at the Stadio Flaminio, having been cited for punching Stephen Jones. Bergamasco was to get another long suspension this time round. The match ended with players squaring up to each other, and Bergamasco was subsequently charged with eye-gouging Lee Byrne, something he admitted at the disciplinary hearing. He received a 13-week lay-off. The second row Carlo Del Fava was also cited, accused of kneeing Stephen Jones in the head early in the game, but the case was thrown out.

The second row Ian Gough had said about Mauro Bergamasco before the match, 'I am sure the referees are aware of the temperamental capabilities that he produces in games. If someone puts a cheap shot in, then punching them back and things like that is not what we are about. But we will go toe-to-toe with any team and always look to get on the front foot. We don't believe in backing down. That does not mean being indisciplined, because having someone sent to the sin-bin gives the advantage to the other side.'

Gatland insisted that selection for the following game in Ireland would hinge on the first three matches, not how Wales fared against Italy. 'We have made a fair few changes, and if it does not work, I will be the first afterwards to say that we made a mistake,' he said. 'We have made some good calls so far, but hindsight is a wonderful thing. It is not just about the short term, even though we are trying to win the Six Nations. It is important that we look to the medium and long terms and see what depth we have and what happens if we pick up some injuries. There are other things than winning the Italian match, and what we are trying to say is that we have faith in the whole squad as we look ahead to Dublin. The guys who started the first two games will be in the box seat for Croke Park, because they have produced good results, but the task of the ones who have come in is to put them under pressure.'

The centre Tom Shanklin was winning his 50th cap. Like his co-centre Gavin Henson, triumph in 2005 was followed by despair. He went to New Zealand with the Lions that summer but suffered a knee injury, which he aggravated when he returned for Cardiff Blues in the domestic season. As he started the long road to rehabilitation, he was warned that he might never play again. 'It will be the proudest day in my career,' he said. 'The fact I will be reaching the landmark in Cardiff will make it all the more special. There was a time when I did not know if I would win another cap, let alone reach 50. The thing about being a player is that you know the next game could be your last. I am just glad to be in the side still, because I struggled for a while against Scotland. It was good to start a game with Gavin Henson again. I like to run angles off him rather than the outside-half, and he provided some lovely touches. He is superb at taking play to the line and making space for others.' The mention of Henson invited comparisons with 2005. 'I will let the papers talk about the prospect of another Grand Slam,' Shanklin said. 'We have to get this game out of the way and then prepare for a tough end to the campaign. We cannot afford to look any further ahead than Italy. We do not have a good recent record against them, and they have given a good account of themselves in their first two matches.'

Shanklin was to score the match-turning try early in the second half, intercepting an ill-advised, floated pass from Masi on the halfway line and sprinting 50 yards to score. Wales had made their customary slow start, but there had been an element of design to it, and their 13–8 interval lead was to be the highest of their campaign. Stephen Jones kicked two early penalties to punish Italian indiscretions at the breakdown, but the crowd was silenced when Wales conceded a try after twelve minutes. The hooker Matthew

Rees threw into a lineout ten yards from his own line, but it went over the head of Gough and into the arms of the Leicester prop Martin Castrogiovanni, who, after overcoming his surprise, took advantage of a disorganised defence to bulldoze his way over.

It was the last time Wales's line was to be breached in the tournament, but in the opening half Italy caused Wales more problems defensively than any other side had or was to. Mallett had chosen an outside-half, Andrea Marcato, to replace the injured David Bortolussi at full-back. He did not compare as a goal-kicker, twice hitting a post to cost his side five points, but Wales struggled to pick up his runs from deep at set-pieces. One move saw Marcato slip through two tackles before the ball found its way to the centre Gonzalo Canale from Masi. He was ten yards from the Wales line moving right and only had to catch the pass to score. But Mauro Bergamasco was in his line of vision, and Canale was momentarily distracted. He dropped the ball and with it the chance to give Italy the lead. Mallett was caught on camera leaving his seat and repeatedly thumping the wall of his hospitality box in frustration. Within five minutes, Wales had scored their first try when Henson sent in Byrne at the corner after a cross-field move.

There may have been a lack of activity on the scoreboard, but Wales were applying body blows to the Italians by not kicking the ball dead, and it was the work they did in the opening 40 minutes that set the foundation for what was to come. Italy's kicking game was poor, and they came in at the interval having made 73 tackles compared to Wales's 26. Their expected superiority in the scrum did not materialise, and if Gatland had one thing in common with Mike Ruddock, it was his ability to neutralise the strengths of opponents and to turn a perceived weakness in his own team into a virtue.

'Our plan was to keep the ball on the park for most of the game, because we knew Italy would tire,' said Shaun Edwards. 'The tactics worked an absolute dream, and we ran away with the game in the final ten minutes. My abiding memory of the game was Ian Gough at the final whistle. He came into the dressing-room ashen-faced. He had pushed his body to the limit and was absolutely spent. He had hit 47 rucks, defended well and shown what a team game rugby is. Gethin Jenkins also hit more than 40 rucks, and their unselfish work meant the backs were on their feet, rather than in rucks, ready to do their job – scoring tries. We all like to see the guys such as Shane Williams dazzle, but they cannot do it without the work of the Ian Goughs of this world.'

Shanklin's try came within one minute of the restart, and shortly afterwards the centre Mirco Bergamasco was sent to the sin-bin for slowing the ball down at a ruck, giving Stephen Jones his fourth penalty of the afternoon. Jones then showed that when it came to creative ability Hook was not on his own as an outside-half by deftly releasing Shane Williams for the wing's third try of the tournament, edging him closer to Gareth Thomas's record. Wales were by now rampant, playing with the freedom and verve that characterised the 2005 Grand Slam side, and Byrne and Williams both scored their second tries of the match. What was also notable was that Stephen Jones and Hook, after he had come on in the 69th minute, kicked all their goals, nine out of nine between them. It followed 100 per cent records against England and Scotland and meant that Wales had landed every one of their penalty attempts and conversions, a stark contrast to the World Cup match against Fiji in Nantes when Hook missed a penalty virtually in front of the posts that he would have been expected to land with his left foot. Wales's kicking game, out of hand and from the floor, was unrecognisable from the year before. It highlighted not only the surge in confidence that results had given them, but it was also a reward for the effort put in on the training field.

'I don't think the first half was disappointing for us, even though the sides were close on the scoreboard,' said Gatland afterwards. 'The hard work we put in then allowed us to up the tempo after the interval. The good thing about this squad is that you do not have to repeat yourself; they pick things up very quickly. I cannot speak too highly about the way they have applied themselves. You are not going to dominate a game for 80 minutes. It is a question of how you react when you are under pressure, and considering the short amount of time we have been together, I am pleased at how things are going. In all three games, there have been things we have needed to address at half-time, and we have done that. We have been asking the players to play a completely different game. It is very tough on them and requires that they work incredibly hard, but you have to demand that in international rugby. I thought we were outstanding in the second half. It was important to score so many points, because even if we lose to Ireland we will still have a chance of winning the title on points difference if we beat France on the final day. When I was with Ireland, we twice missed out on the top spot because our points difference was not as good as England's and France's, so to win by so many sets us up well. We are in a reasonable position, but the good thing is that our destiny is in our own hands. We have the opportunity to set ourselves up for the Triple Crown and the championship, and I admit I am a little surprised about that.'

Wales won the second period 34–0 and in doing so recorded the highest winning margin in a Six Nations match at the Millennium Stadium: 39 points. The match statistics did not lie and showed the extent of the home side's dominance: one hundred and forty passes completed compared to seventy-one; twelve line breaks against four; fifty-six tackles put in as opposed to Italy's one hundred and thirty-five; and Wales were in possession of the ball for nearly thirty-two minutes compared with Italy's twenty-two. The top five tacklers were all Italian, and the four players who carried the ball most often were all Welsh. But the most significant statistic was that Wales only once kicked the ball to touch, other than from a penalty. They put boot to ball on 30 occasions, virtually always kicking it long and keeping it in play. 'Wales's kicking game was very good,' said Mallett. 'There was only one team in it in the second half, and it was always going to be a question of how many tries they scored. It is hard to gauge from this game just how good Wales are, because we were not competitive enough, but they will certainly gain in confidence from it, and in guys like Henson, Shanklin and Shane Williams they have players who can make a real difference. They and France are the best attacking teams in the tournament.'

It was a day that again showed the difference in Byrne from the season before. Whether he was fielding high kicks, getting Italy players scrambling back in their own half to field his raking left-footed punts, making tackles or finishing off moves, he looked as if he had been a fixture in the side for years, and full-back was a problem position for Gatland no more. 'Lee has hardly put a foot wrong,' said Gatland. 'His kicking game is great, and he is superb in the air. It is nice to see a player who is in such good form so relaxed yet so confident. People had said to me shortly after I arrived that he was a player who blew hot and cold and was a bit shaky confidence wise. I am not one who has preconceived ideas about players: I make up my own mind. I watched him play for the Ospreys, and he was superb, and he has been absolutely brilliant for us, the best full-back in the competition at the moment.'

Byrne was not comfortable dwelling on his own display. 'The result was far more important than my personal display,' he said. 'As a team, we are getting what we deserve. A lot has been said about magic team talks, but it is simply the case that we have a game plan and we are sticking to it. We wanted to keep the ball on the park, because we knew Italy had a strong driving-lineout game, and they only had eight throw-ins all afternoon. When we went to their changing-room to swap jerseys, that is all they were on about – how few lineouts we gave them. They were a tired team at the end. We knew they would be hard to subdue for the first 40 minutes and then it was going to be a case of our fitness telling.'

A problem for Gatland now was coping with public expectation. 'Just as it was not the end of the world when we lost to Fiji, neither should people now believe that we are world beaters,' said Mark Jones. 'This regime is only three games old, and there is still an awfully long way to go in this championship. The best thing so far is that there has been a change to the way we prepare. You hear the word intensity used a lot, but that does not explain things fully. We do less, but it is of massive benefit to us and ensures we stay fresh. There will be talk about the Triple Crown with Ireland our next match, but our focus can only be on winning the game. We are confident, but we are not overconfident. Plenty of good Wales teams have come unstuck in Dublin in the past, but no one has ever played at Croke Park before.'

Like Mark Jones, Gough reflected on how quickly fortunes could change. 'We went through some hard times in the Six Nations last year,' he said. 'It does not make for a pleasant experience when you are shunned at airports, and that memory ensures that we will only take things one step at a time now. We are coming on, but there are still aspects to our game which need to be ironed out. We are not a complete team by any stretch of the imagination. We have to keep remembering that we are where we are because of all the hard work we have put in in the build-up to matches. We have to keep doing that, and what we have to take out of this game, good victory though it was, is to work out how we can become more effective.'

A few hours after Wales had beaten Italy, Ireland found a semblance of their old form as they overcame an uncertain start to overwhelm Scotland at Croke Park 34–13. The pressure was off Eddie O'Sullivan, who had succeeded Gatland in 2001, but only for the moment. And as the streets around the Millennium Stadium started to clear late in the evening, England were on their way to defeating France in Paris for the second time in five months. It meant that only Wales could win the Grand Slam, although Ireland, England and France retained an interest in the title. A year before at this stage, Wales had been confronting the prospect of a whitewash after losing their opening three matches. 'We have created an atmosphere in this squad, and we have to keep it going,' said Ryan Jones. 'It's all about Dublin now.'

The Six Nations was to take a break for another weekend before the final two rounds were played, and the attention in Wales and Ireland turned to the reunion of O'Sullivan and Gatland. 'I am sure I am going to be asked about Warren a lot in the next couple of weeks,' said O'Sullivan after the victory over Scotland. 'He has got Wales on the right foot, and they are moving forwards. We saw in 2005 that when Wales get a good start in the Six Nations their confidence shoots up and they become a real handful. We are seeing the same sort of pep in their step, and Warren has induced it very quickly. But they have got to come to Dublin. This is our backyard, and we are not going to give up anything very easily. It's all to play for now for us, and we still have a chance of winning the Triple Crown.'

Gatland was not going to name his team early for Dublin, and he had a week to ponder over a number of keenly contested positions: Jones or Hook at outside-half, Mike Phillips or Dwayne Peel at scrum-half, Gethin Jenkins or Duncan Jones at loose-head prop, Matthew Rees or Huw Bennett at hooker? Peel, who in 2005 had been regarded as the leading scrum-half in the world, started against Italy but was replaced early in the second half after taking a blow on the head and suffering blurred vision. His departure coincided with Wales establishing their superiority, and Phillips did not believe the selectors had a choice to make for the Ireland match. 'To be honest, I do not know what more I have to do,' he said. 'I was really happy with the way I played in the first two games, and today I thought I did more than enough. I cannot really produce any more. It was not long ago that there was only one choice at number 9; people are debating the position now, and that means I have closed the gap. I do not see any reason why we cannot go out to Dublin and put on a really good performance. We should be really confident now, because there are things that we are doing very well.'

Two days after the victory over Italy, it was announced that the American rock band REM would play at the Millennium Stadium the following August, but there were no shiny, happy rugby followers in Wales losing their religion.

6

··

THAT FELLOW
EDWARDS

True sport is always a duel: a duel with nature, with
one's own fear, with one's own fatigue, a duel in
which body and mind are strengthened.

Yevgeny Yevtushenko

11 APRIL 1983. ENGLAND ARE PLAYING WALES IN AN
Under-16 schools international at Bristol. Their
captain is a 16-year-old centre who, three days before,
had led England's Under-16 rugby league team in an
international. Shaun Edwards scores his side's opening try
at Bristol, but it is a Nigerian wing, Obi Egbuna, who
proves the match-winner with a 50-yard try as England
edge home 14–13.

Packing down at tight-head prop for Wales was David

Young, who would go on to play for Swansea, Cardiff, Wales and the Lions before moving to rugby league. He scored the final try of the game, and when Edwards became Wales's defence coach at the start of 2008, Young was in charge of one of the country's four regions, Cardiff Blues. 'What I remember most about that day is that Wales scrummaged us off the park and we hardly saw the ball,' recalled Edwards. 'Hardly a surprise with Dai Young in their front row. The strange thing was, given the reputation of the two countries at the time, that we were more dangerous behind, and we scored a couple of tries against the run of play. I enjoyed playing union, but I was born and bred in Wigan, and I was only ever going to have a playing career in league.' His father, Jack, had played for Warrington before suffering a spinal injury and having to retire at the age of twenty-four, one year before Edwards was born.

Later in 1983, on his 17th birthday, Edwards signed for Wigan for what was a reported record salary of £35,000. The event was televised live on the BBC's north-west news programme from Edwards's parents' house, and it was to be the start of a remarkable career: when Wales won the 2008 Six Nations championship, it was the 25th major trophy Edwards had enjoyed in 25 years in professional rugby as a player and a coach. 'The crux of the matter was that I did not get all the money at once. It was spread over four years,' said Edwards in an interview with the *Daily Telegraph*. 'All the old pros thought I was getting that straight away, so they tried to make sure I earned it. It was no place for the faint-hearted. I got bashed to hell. Within ten games, I broke my nose, got a tooth knocked out and had some fifteen stitches in my face. Welcome to rugby league. I thought, "I can't do this for another ten or twelve years," but fear of failure was a massive driving force for me.' Fear of the consequences of failure was to prove a massive driving force for the Wales squad when Edwards arrived to join Warren Gatland in January 2008.

Edwards, a scrum-half in league, although he appeared at stand-off, centre and full-back at various times, played 467 times for Wigan between 1983 and 1996, scoring 1,146 points. In 1992, he scored ten tries against Swinton in a Lancashire Cup match. He had a stint with Balmain Tigers in 1989 and two spells at London Broncos with a season at Bradford in between before retiring as a player in 2000 after five hundred and eighty-four appearances and thirty-six caps for Great Britain, four as captain. He won eight successive Challenge Cup ties with Wigan at Wembley, playing in every one of a record forty-three consecutive unbeaten matches in the tournament. In total, he won nine Challenge Cups with the club and eight league titles before leaving after falling out with the club's then coach Eric Ashton, who died the week after Wales won the 2008 Grand Slam. Edwards had had a son, James, with his partner Heather Small, a singer with the group M People, and he wanted to spend some time in London with them. Ashton refused. 'I was pretty upset,' said Edwards. 'In my heart of hearts, I did not want to leave, but I felt I needed to make a go of it with James's mum. We were living in a one-room apartment in London with Heather's mum and the baby, and it was a pretty crowded environment. It did not work out, but we are still close friends.'

Edwards made his 11th and last Challenge Cup final appearance for London Broncos in 1999, the last to be held at Wembley before the stadium was rebuilt. He had only been on the losing side in a Wembley final once, on his first visit to the ground as a player in 1984, but the Broncos were to lose by a record 52–16.

When Edwards joined Warren Gatland at Wales, he told the players that there would be no excuses for anyone not joining the defensive line, not even a serious injury. 'I suppose a broken leg might be different, but they could still hop up,' he said. As a player, he never surrendered to pain. After ten minutes in the 1990 Challenge Cup final against Warrington, he was hit hard in the face and needed prolonged treatment. He had suffered a triple fracture of the eye socket and a fractured cheekbone, but he played on for the remaining 70 minutes, only going to hospital after the end of the match. 'It was a pretty painful win,' he wrote in his column in *The Guardian* in 2007. 'I'll never forget bumping around in the ambulance as I was being driven to hospital: I thought my head was going to explode and wanted them to operate to stop the pain; because I had been concussed, all they could do was give me two paracetamols.' A poster on the newspaper's website recalled, 'He played with his usual intensity despite the injury. When the final whistle blew, the other Wigan players started to celebrate, but Shaun just collapsed. People talk about toughness in sport, but that for me was the ultimate example.'

'As soon as it happened, Shaun told me he thought he had broken his cheekbone,' said Edwards's half-back partner at Wigan, Andy Gregory. 'He said he would be fine, and he carried on making heavy tackles and knocking blokes down, even though he was in agony. It was incredible.' Three weeks before, he had played on against Leeds despite breaking a bone in his hand.

Edwards was renowned for his intensity and single-mindedness, driven hard as a youngster and as a professional by his father, yet there was another, softer side to him that only those who got to know him came to appreciate. 'I must admit that I could not stand Giz [the nickname Edwards was given shortly after he had arrived at Wigan, derived from a character called Gizmo in the 1984 comic horror movie, *Gremlins*] when I joined Wigan from Oldham,' wrote the former prop Barrie McDermott in his autobiography, *Made for Rugby*:

> That quickly turned to admiration. He was the first Wigan player to come up to me and wish me all the best, and when I was a young professional trying to make a name for myself, he taught me a lot. He was a natural winner, a great competitor and a fantastic leader. He won every honour in the game, and his record speaks for itself: he was one of the very few stars who changed the way his position was played.

Edwards senior admitted that he had never let up on his son. 'I did not push Shaun, I kicked him,' he said in a book about Wigan's golden era, *Blood, Mud and Glory*. 'It was obvious that he had natural talent as a youngster. That alone is not enough, however. He has worked very hard and has always had a ruthless winning streak.' Edwards was always in the top half of his class at school, until he reached the age of 14 and fixated on becoming a professional rugby league player. He ended up becoming the most decorated player in British rugby league history, and in 1996 he was awarded the OBE.

After retiring from playing at the beginning of 2000 because of a chronic knee injury, Edwards, a devout Catholic, found himself out of work. He wanted to get into coaching, having passed his rugby league coaching exams a few weeks after his 18th birthday, but there were no openings for him in the south of England. He twice flew to Australia, the second time at his own expense, to seek advice from the Brisbane Broncos coach Wayne Bennett and then visited the United States. 'Wayne taught me about how coaches handle themselves,' he said. 'I also watched a couple of Clive Woodward's training sessions with England. Ellery Hanley [who was in the same Wigan team as Edwards] was the defence coach of the England A side, and he got me in.'

Edwards then went on a pilgrimage to Jerusalem with his mother, Phyllis, where he met two Irish Franciscan monks, Father John and Father Eamonn, who became big influences on him. 'I told them I would like to do something to help the poor, and Father Eamonn suggested that I offer my services to the sisters running a homeless shelter in Southall. I just went down and took it from there.' He was still looking for jobs and doing charity work when Hanley invited him to watch a match at Wasps.

'Wasps had always been my rugby union team,' said Edwards. 'I am not sure why. You know how it is: you adopt teams in American football or Spanish soccer, and I always looked out for Wasps. I played against them in a sevens tournament once for Wigan and remember them being quite aggressive in the tunnel before we went on and me thinking that I quite liked them.' He had an offer to join Warrington's coaching staff, but he wanted to remain in London and went along with Offiah to watch Wasps. 'I always fancied a crack at rugby union, but no opportunities had come along. As it turned out, when I did get my chance, it was for less money than I would have had at Warrington and the contract was shorter, but it was exactly what I had been looking for.'

It was the early spring in 2001. Wasps, league champions in 1997 and the domestic cup winners in 1999 and 2000, were starting to decline. Their director of rugby at the time, Nigel Melville, remembers the first occasion he met Edwards. 'I arrived in the changing-room at the end of the match to address the players, and there was Shaun sitting with them, all pumped up and excited at the win. Shaun was infectious, and after he told me that he was interested in doing a bit of coaching, I invited him to attend a few sessions. He said he had been offered a contract by Warrington but wanted to stay close to his son in London, and I thought, given the way he had interacted with the players so well, that it was worth having a look at him. I can still recall the first training session he attended: he walked out in his shorts and rugby league kit, but minus socks, and he was holding a piece of paper. I am not sure that the players had a clue who he was and found his strong Lancashire accent difficult to understand. It was hilarious watching the players try to do things with the ball that only Shaun could.

'He did some handling and ball-manipulation skills and then we moved on to contact. We were short of a tackle shield holder, and the next thing I knew there he was at the end of the line, shield in hand. Approaching him at pace were Simon Shaw and Lawrence Dallaglio, not the smallest forwards on our books. Before I could say anything, Shaun was lying on his back with a bemused look on his face. Eventually, he got to his feet, threw down his shield and said, "I think somebody else better hold this." In the next few weeks, he questioned more or less everything we did. Why did we always stand so close? Why did we always spin a pass, no matter how far it had to travel? Why did we kick the way we did? On one occasion,

I saw he was about to get involved in lineout drills and, for once, asked him to back off. However, no matter how much he questioned our very being, it was never offensive. He is a people person and likes to use the word why. Added to that, he is the most generous guy I know, and over Christmas you will probably find him working in a soup kitchen. Wasps were very quickly won over by him: his prompting kept moving us forward, and his enthusiasm made it easy to try out a stream of new ideas. His background commanded respect, and it was somehow no surprise when he told me that he had lost his front teeth at the age of four when, playing rugby in his living room, he had slipped and crashed head first into a table leg.'

No pain, no gain was Edwards's mantra. 'The way Shaun won over our outside-half Alex King revealed everything about him,' said Melville, who in 2006 became the chief executive of USA Rugby. 'They had seemed like chalk and cheese and on totally different wavelengths – the one public-school educated and the other a working-class hero – until Alex picked up an injury shortly before an important game. He could not raise his arms above shoulder height and was going to cry off, and we faced losing him for the rest of the season. Shaun said that he had had the same injury before an international between Great Britain and Australia. The medics told him that he required immediate shoulder surgery, but Shaun devised a way of playing. "I wasn't going to miss that game," he said. The following day, he turned up to training with an old leather shoulder harness and proceeded to strap it on to Alex. By the time all the tape had been applied, Alex is trussed up like a chicken bound for the oven and not looking particularly impressed. As Shaun took a step backwards to admire his handiwork, Alex asks, "What happens if someone kicks the ball over my head?"

'"Get someone else to catch it," comes the reply.

'There is a short pause before Alex continues, "How long exactly did you wear this contraption for?"

'"About 12 years," says Shaun.'

A year later, Melville left Wasps for Gloucester. The London club had slumped to the bottom of the Premiership, and Warren Gatland took over as director of rugby, three months after being sacked by Ireland, with Edwards by now the head coach. It was the start of one of the most successful partnerships in English club rugby, one which was to have an immediate impact on the international game in 2008. 'People say that Warren and I are different characters, which is why we work so well together, but I am not so sure about that,' said Edwards. 'It is certainly not a case of good cop, bad cop. Warren is never afraid to say what he thinks to anyone. We hit it off straight away, off the field as well as on it. I am never afraid to give him the benefit of my opinion, and we have disagreements, but his decision is final, and I will always back him to the hilt. He's the boss, but if I feel strongly about something, he will always support me. He gave me confidence when he arrived at Wasps. I had wanted to introduce the blitz defence but had not felt comfortable doing it on my own. I could not understand why, with the ruck-and-maul law, which meant players only had to stand behind the feet of their hindmost player at the breakdown, everyone did not adopt the system. Warren thought it was a great idea, and we went for it. The rest is history.'

Wasps won six of the final eight matches of the 2001–02 season to clamber to safety and beyond. Twelve months later, they were champions and winners of the European Challenge Cup. In his autobiography, *It's in the Blood: My*

Life, Lawrence Dallaglio, the Wasps captain between 1999 and 2008, wrote:

> Nigel Melville might not thank me for saying this, but I think his bringing Shaun and Warren to the club was as great a contribution as anything he did for Wasps. Shane has the same common-sense approach to life that Warren has. He did not come in shouting about how much we had to learn from rugby league but would instead point to a ball and start talking. 'Same oval shape in league and union,' he would say, 'same green grass, same objective of grounding the ball over the other team's line.' They say an open mind is the definition of intelligence, and if that's true, Shaun must be very bright. There is so much about him that players respond to. The thing I noticed immediately was that most of what he did on the training ground was relevant to what you would do on the Saturday. You weren't doing bullshit drills or moves that bore no relation to the reality of a match. Neither did he waffle on or use corporate jargon to make a point. He would show us something as basic as touching a ball down correctly when scoring a try and have us do a drill that reinforced that tactical aspect of a game.
>
> One of the things about Shaun is that he's odd, but interestingly odd. You meet him, he talks a lot of sense and he makes you want to know more about him, but he doesn't reveal everything. It is not like you are going to know him after three or four meetings. What makes him fascinating is that he looks at situations his way, and although he is

a very humble bloke, he is not afraid to call things as he sees them . . . He is the heartbeat of Wasps, the engine that drives things on the training ground. When he is referred to as the defensive coach, that is an insult. He's defence, attack, tactics, strategy, psychology, lots of things. I think Nigel Melville saw how effective Warren and Shaun would be together. Although they were from two very different places, Warren a New Zealander and Shaun from the north of England, they were like two peas in a pod. Neither sought the limelight, and when they walked into a team room, players quickly realised they were not there to promote themselves. They both enjoyed a drink and an occasional bet on the horses, and they had no desire to push themselves above the players.

There was a certain apprehension among the Wales squad when they learned that Edwards would be teaming up with Gatland again at the start of 2008. They knew of his reputation and, with his bald head and a face that told the story of hundreds of matches and was rarely caught on camera smiling, did not have to be told that they could not expect the arrival of a holiday-camp attendant. Wales's new backs coach Robert Howley, who had played at Wasps under the pair, did nothing to ease the tension. But while Edwards demands high standards, he is anything but a martinet. Dallaglio wrote:

Shaun is a very human, blue-collar sort of a bloke. He would have the backs in early one morning and have them work incredibly hard on one aspect of their play; at the end of the session, he would invite them to a diner in Ealing for breakfast and pay the bill. It was his way of showing the players that he was more than a coaching machine: he was also a human being, and he enjoyed the *craic* and a bit of banter.

Edwards not only introduced Wales to his tradition of singing after winning but also showed he had bottle. 'We all dread going into the video-analysis room on the Monday or Tuesday after a game, because we know we will not get any pats on the back from Shaun,' said the full-back Lee Byrne. 'He surprised us after our first match against England by coming into the room armed with two bottles of champagne, which he gave to the player he thought had the most outstanding game, Mike Phillips, and I got them after the Scotland victory. But that is the only smile you get out of him. After the presentation, it is head down as he goes through all the bad points.'

Gatland and Edwards were together at Wasps for three full seasons. They won the Premiership – which at the start of the 2002–03 campaign had adopted a play-off format to determine the champions – three times, starting with victory over Melville's Gloucester in the 2003 play-off final, supplementing it with the European Challenge Cup in the same year and the Heineken Cup in 2004. Dallaglio personified the two men on the pitch, never taking a step backwards, and the three formed a close working relationship. They had all been affected by personal tragedy. When he was coaching Galwegians in Ireland in the 1990s, Gatland's daughter Shauna was born with spina bifida and died at the age of four months. In 1989, Dallaglio's sister Francesca, a 19-year-old student ballerina, died when the pleasure boat

Marchioness sank on the River Thames following a collision with a dredger. In February 2003, Edwards's 20-year-old brother Billy Joe, a player in Wigan's academy, was killed in a car accident. When Wales faced England at Twickenham on the opening day of the 2008 Six Nations, it would have been Billy Joe's 25th birthday.

'They say time heals, but it doesn't really,' said Edwards. 'Billy Joe's death was the biggest event in my life. When I received the telephone call telling me what had happened, I knew that my life would never be the same again. I do not know what I would have done had I been unemployed. I am someone who needs to have his mind occupied. I spoke to Billy Joe as I walked around the pitch at the Millennium Stadium before the game against France. I had asked him for a bit of help at half-time at Twickenham. I appreciate now that rugby is not about life and death, even if I am still intense about it. It is a game, and if we lose, I am not as devastated about it as I was before Billy Joe died. Lawrence knew what I was going through, having lost his sister, and there is a special bond between us. He is almost like family to me.'

When Gatland left Wasps in 2005 to return to Waikato, Ian McGeechan took his place. A highly experienced coach, having taken the Lions on three tours and having had two stints coaching Scotland, leading them to the Grand Slam in 1990, he recognised that he did not have to change much at Wasps and quickly forged a strong relationship with Edwards. Wasps won the Powergen Cup in 2006, defeating Llanelli Scarlets in the final at Twickenham, the first year the tournament had been opened to the Welsh regions, and in 2007 Wasps claimed the Heineken Cup for the second time, again at Twickenham, after beating

Leicester in the final. Edwards had been to English rugby's headquarters for six finals (Wasps won the 2003 European Challenge Cup final in Reading) and been on the winning side each time.

'I got on well with Shaun from the start,' said McGeechan. 'Like him, I was brought up in the north of England, and I had come across characters similar to him before. The first thing you get to appreciate is that he is an exceptional coach. You only have to look at the fact that Wales only conceded two tries in their five Six Nations matches after Shaun's arrival to appreciate that. It is not just his ideas that are good, it is the way he can put them across to a group of players from scratch. It is a measure of the man, because you have to be pretty special to do that. It is easy for players to relate to him, because he is honest and straightforward. Players quickly understand what is expected of them: they are given a role, and if they blow it, watch out. He sets high standards, but he is also a very kind, considerate man. He thinks about people and what he does. Away from rugby, he does a lot of thoughtful things, and there is a real depth to the man. He is very quick to detect when a player is having problems, whether related to rugby or not, and he will take them out for a coffee or go around to their house for a chat.'

When Gatland agreed to take charge of Wales, he wanted Edwards and Howley to join him on the management team. He gave the Welsh Rugby Union a commitment that he would have some Welsh coaches on his staff, and, as well as Howley, he retained the forwards coach Robin McBryde and kicking coach Neil Jenkins, both of whom had been part of Gareth Jenkins's regime. While Edwards was interested both in linking up with Gatland again and fulfilling his ambition of working with an international side, he was fired by patriotism and would always admit to an interviewer that one of his ambitions was to coach England. Gatland started work with Wales on 1 December, and the Welsh Rugby Union had already begun talking to Wasps and Cardiff Blues about securing Edwards and Howley respectively. Howley was under contract to the Blues for another two years, and a compromise was eventually reached that would allow the former scrum-half to be with Wales when they were in camp for the Six Nations and return to the Blues for the rest of the season before starting work with Wales on a permanent basis.

The negotiations over Edwards were more protracted and complicated. England had reached the World Cup final against all the odds, but the Rugby Football Union had decided to conduct an exhaustive review into the national management team, which was headed by Brian Ashton, like Gatland a former Ireland coach. His two assistants were John Wells (forwards) and Mike Ford (defence). Ford had been a teammate of Edwards's at Wigan, occupying the scrum-half spot when the teenager arrived at Central Park and forcing him to play initially at full-back. England's feat in reaching the final for the second successive time had not led to a clamour for Ashton to be knighted; England had been thrashed 36–0 at the group stage by South Africa and had to beat Samoa and Tonga, neither totally convincingly, to get into the last eight. It was when the pressure was on them that England responded, but they showed little in the way of creativity as they squeezed past Australia and France to get to the final, where they were beaten in a kicking contest by South Africa.

There were many in England, at club level and on the

RFU, who felt that the national squad players were not being stimulated enough, although the questionnaires filled in by those who were involved in the World Cup showed a large measure of support for the management team. Edwards's name was being mentioned as a potential head coach, never mind defence coach. When interviewed by the media, he said he did not anticipate England making any changes, because they had reached a World Cup final. When the RFU's director of elite rugby, Rob Andrew, made his recommendations to the union's management board, he argued for Ashton, Wells and Ford to stay put. The vote went unanimously in his favour, although it was agreed that, looking forward, a team manager would be appointed after the Six Nations and an extra backs coach would be considered. Even though the coaches were kept on, on one-year rolling contracts, Andrew said the intention was to keep Ashton and his assistants in place to the 2011 World Cup. The door appeared to have been slammed shut in Edwards's face.

As soon as Andrew's review was concluded, Wales stepped up negotiations with Wasps. Edwards, even when he was being linked with England, had always said that while he wanted to become involved in the international game, he was only prepared to do so on a part-time basis. He would not, under any circumstances, give up his job with Wasps. 'They are my family,' he was fond of saying. Premier Rugby, the umbrella organisation representing all 12 Premiership clubs, had a policy that prohibited club coaches from taking part-time roles with England at any level, the aim being to prevent anyone from gaining an advantage over coaching rivals by having a chance to tap up players. The policy was extended after the end of the 2008

Six Nations to cover all other countries, on the grounds that it was wrong for English clubs to have a sanction that could benefit other unions at England's expense; it was not applied retrospectively, meaning Edwards was free to continue with Wales.

The RFU maintains that it did approach Edwards when Andy Robinson was fired as head coach towards the end of 2006, but it was not able to bring anyone into the national set-up on a part-time basis because of the Premier Rugby rule, and Edwards was not prepared to leave Wasps. But as Wales became more and more confident of signing up Edwards, so the RFU became concerned about losing one of their brightest and youngest coaching talents, not least because of the adverse public reaction it would generate. One day in December, when Edwards had decided to sign with Wales, having reached an agreement with Wasps, and was preparing to announce the fact in his column in *The Guardian*, he received a call from Kevin Bowring, the RFU's director of elite coaching, asking him to hold fire.

The RFU had previously asked Edwards to take charge of England Saxons, the new name for what had been England A, promising to get the part-time rule waived, but he would not have been allowed to appoint his own coaching team or have the final say on selection. The post also commanded a relatively meagre salary, not that that was an issue for a man not driven by money. Bowring eventually came back with a modified offer, but it still amounted to taking charge of the Saxons on the terms of others. If the RFU thought it was being seen to be doing something, it was also patently obvious that that something did not add up to very much. Gatland could not believe his fortune, but it was the other member of the Wasps triumvirate, McGeechan, who played the crucial role in securing the deal that took Edwards to Wales.

'Shaun had been at Wasps for seven years and had achieved considerable success,' said McGeechan. 'I felt the time was right for him to test himself at international level. He needed that extra challenge, but equally Wasps did not want to lose him. I had to persuade the board at Wasps that he would be able to fill the two jobs at the same time. Some directors were concerned that Shaun would end up being overloaded and that the club could suffer, but that is where the understanding I had with Warren came to the fore. I am not sure the arrangement could have been worked out if either Warren or I had not been involved. The three of us knew that we could make it work, and there was trust on both sides, coupled with a desire to make sure that both Wales and Wasps benefited from it. England did not see it the same way, and you would have to say, after the way the 2008 Six Nations panned out, that they did miss a trick. There is a strong Wasps link at Wales with Rob Howley and Rhys Long [notational analyst] also part of the management team. The move has been terrific for Shaun. He has long desired to be part of the Lions' management team in South Africa in 2009, and he knew that to fulfil that ambition he needed to gain international experience.

'I was not surprised that the Wales players took so quickly to Shaun. He is someone you might not work out at once, but it does not take individuals long to realise that what he is all about is improving them as rugby players. Everything he does is for a reason, and that is why players always have a huge loyalty to him. I would go out of my way to do anything for him, and I think I showed that in the talks with Wales. I did everything I could to convince the Wasps board that the arrangement would work, and the reason I did that was because we were talking about Shaun Edwards. You cannot count the pluses he brings to a team, and I think the way Gavin Henson has reacted to Shaun's arrival says it all. A player who had appeared to have lost his way was made one of the defence captains and responded with some outstanding performances. That is what Shaun inspires from his players.'

After Martyn Williams had scored the try against France that wrapped up the 2008 Grand Slam, the big screens at the ground showed the Wales management sitting in their hospitality box. 'Edwards is a Welsh name,' sang the crowd. Edwards does have some Welsh ancestry, a great-grandfather, but he had stronger connections with Ireland through his maternal grandmother, and in the dying days of his rugby league career in 1998 he played for Ireland in their first full international, against France, although only 1,500 turned up at Tolka Park in Dublin to watch. 'I felt more and more Irish as the game went on,' he said. He did not return home to London for another four days. One member of the crowd was the former world boxing champion Steve Collins, an Irishman who had been a long-time admirer of Edwards and was keen to meet him. The two are now close friends.

Before Wasps played, and beat, Munster in the 2004 Heineken Cup semi-final at Lansdowne Road in Dublin, the club's England full-back Josh Lewsey revealed how Edwards motivated his players in the build-up to the game by writing each member of the backline messages of reassurance. 'There are usually a few spelling mistakes, but once you have picked your way through them, what you get are words of wisdom,' said Lewsey. 'They are not really to do with rugby, more with your life in general. Coming from a guy who has been as successful as him, I do take note. Shaun's great strength is reading individuals and knowing what makes people tick.' One of Wasps' props that day, the Irishman Peter Bracken, developed the theme. 'It is like he can see through the player and actually see the person behind,' he said. 'Having the key to someone's emotions unleashes a better-prepared player. He once said that all Celtic players have a natural aggression and that sometimes we need to psyche ourselves down almost. He would be trying to gee up other guys by shouting and roaring and then whisper to me, "That does not apply to you." He does know what makes every player tick, and while he would lambaste you at times, it was never for the sake of it, and he would take you aside afterwards. You wouldn't make the same mistake again. He wasn't afraid to show his emotions.'

The Wales outside-half Stephen Jones said it had not taken the squad long to appreciate the quality and value of Edwards's input: 'We all knew about his reputation and the fantastic success he had enjoyed as a player and as a coach, but what no one was really prepared for was the intensity that he and Warren brought to training. You are put under pressure, and you have to react. The way he puts things across is very clever and precise, and everything he talks about is relevant to the game coming up. It is not just a matter of ticking boxes; he hits you with facts. I respect everything that he says and feel that if I had an issue I could go to him without any problem to talk about it. He is not the "it's my way or the highway" type of coach. He likes to be challenged, and he made an immediate impact with us.'

After the end of the 2008 Six Nations campaign, Edwards was interviewed on the BBC's *Inside Sport*, relaxing in the informal environment of a wine bar after Wasps had defeated London Irish in Reading the day after Wales's victory over France. He described himself as a 'pretty boring person', driven as he was by a saying he brought to Wasps: 'Are your opponents working harder than you?' Boring is the last word to stick on Edwards, a man who was single-minded as a player but who has become more rounded since hanging up his boots. 'I like reading and watching the History Channel,' he said. 'I have seen a few programmes on the Great Wars lately. There is a cenotaph near where I live, and I often go there to say a prayer for the guys who fell. There was so much horror in those trenches. They must have gone through hell. I now always strive to put others before myself. Whenever I am selfish, I am not happy. You get out of life what you put in. You have to work hard. It is as simple as that. When I was a young player, I did not want to let my parents down. I wanted to make them proud of me. My father was always very stern with me in a rugby sense and used to push me hard. He used to write a report of every match I played in and would always offer constructive criticism. I knew that if he came up and shook my hand after a match that I must have played really well. He has been an inspiration to me.'

The week after Gatland's men had won the Grand Slam, Wales and England met in an Under-16 schools international in Bourgoin in the Four Nations tournament. A Young lined up in the Wales team: it was Thomas, the wing-forward son of David Young, who had opposed Edwards in the same fixture at Bristol 25 years before. At outside-half for England was George Ford, son of the England defence coach Mike, Edwards's former teammate at Wigan. This time Wales won by a point, 13–12.

CASE FOR THE DEFENCE: Shaun Edwards threatens his players with six of the best before the clash against England at Twickenham as prop Duncan Jones looks on.

LEE'S WAY: Full-back Lee Byrne scores Wales's opening try of the campaign to bring his team back into contention at Twickenham after they had been 19–6 down.

SCORE SETTLING: Alun Wyn Jones is the first to congratulate Mike Phillips after the scrum-half scored what turned out to be the match-winning try at Twickenham to end 20 years of misery for Wales at the ground. (© Cleva)

HOME FROM HOME: Coach Warren Gatland won four Twickenham finals out of four with Wasps, and he savours a personal Grand Slam with Wales.

RIGHT HOOK: Outside-half James Hook delivers a knockout blow to Scotland with his side's second try at the Millennium Stadium.

GETTING A LIFT: Second row Ian Gough claims a lineout against Scotland and hit the heights throughout the tournament.

TOUCH AND GO: Wing Shane Williams seals the victory over Scotland with his second try of the game, but there was a dispute over whether he had put a foot in touch.

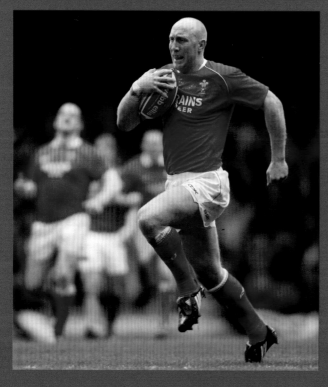

NIFTY FIFTY: Centre Tom Shanklin marks his 50th cap with a 50-metre interception try to break Italy's resistance at the Millennium Stadium.

CENTRE OF ATTENTION: Gavin Henson endured a frustrating period after the 2005 Grand Slam, but Italy were not alone in finding the midfielder passing them by.

RYAN'S EXPRESS: Wales captain Ryan Jones gives his Ireland counterpart Brian O'Driscoll the brush-off at Croke Park, leading from the front as he did throughout.

TRIPLE X FACTOR: Sizzling Shane Williams scores the only try of the game in Dublin, and his first ever against Ireland, as Wales clinch the Triple Crown.

CROKER ROAR: The Wales players celebrate with the Triple Crown trophy in Dublin – next stop, France in Cardiff.

WINNERS TRIPLE CROWN 2008

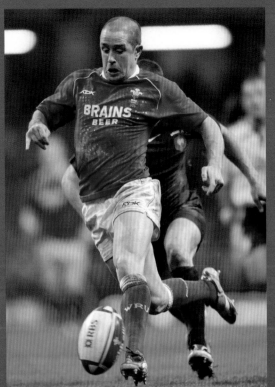

FOOT IN THE DOOR: Shane Williams plays football after seizing on a mistake against France on the way to his 41st and record try for Wales and putting his side on course for the Grand Slam.

SLAM DUNK: Flanker Martyn Williams, the player of the 2005 Six Nations, on his way to sealing Wales's tenth Grand Slam, exactly 100 years after the first.

ROYAL APPROVAL: Prince William applauds as Ryan Jones holds aloft the Six Nations trophy – Warren Gatland and his fellow coaches refused to go on to the podium, telling the players that it was their success.

AIR WE GO: Hooker Huw Bennett appears to use the Six Nations trophy as a guitar as Wales's celebrations start in earnest.

7

....

POWER GAME

To endeavour to forget someone is a certain
way of thinking of nothing else.

Jean de la Bruyere

6 **MARCH 2008. THE BBC'S *SPORTS WALES* PROGRAMME** opens with a feature entitled 'Who Gunned Gats?' It dwells on the circumstances surrounding Warren Gatland's departure as Ireland coach in November 2001, a month after he had guided them to victories in the Six Nations over Wales in Cardiff and England at Lansdowne Road. The matches had been rearranged from earlier in the year because of an outbreak of foot and mouth in Britain. Wales were playing Ireland in Croke Park, Dublin, two days later, a match which would not only see them battle for the Triple Crown, but which would bring Gatland face to face with the man who had succeeded him as the

Ireland head coach, Eddie O'Sullivan, his assistant seven years before.

Some of the characters who had been central in the decision not to offer Gatland a new contract were wheeled out, but O'Sullivan chose to keep his silence. Gatland made a fleeting appearance, stressing the importance of having the undying loyalty of those around you, but there was no evidence that he had been the victim of a conspiracy engineered by his assistant. 'It was a business decision,' said Syd Millar, a key figure in the Irish Rugby Football Union at the time and who went on to become the chairman of the International Rugby Board. It was the biggest setback Gatland had suffered in his coaching career, but he did not hang around feeling sorry for himself and was soon on his way to turn Wasps into a trophy-winning club again.

Gatland had been back to Ireland in 2004 when Wasps played Munster in the Heineken Cup semi-final at Lansdowne Road. In his autobiography, the club captain Lawrence Dallaglio wrote:

> I immediately thought the match would have a special significance for Warren because of the way he had been ditched by Ireland. I did not know the specifics, and in the lead-up to the game I asked him what the story had been over there. 'Look, mate, you don't need to know. Suffice to say, I want to win this ****** game.' I wasn't the only one thinking about Warren going into the game: other players felt the same, and I let it be known in the dressing-room that this was an ideal game for us to repay some of the faith the coach had shown in us. I really do not know what happened with Ireland, but Warren's record

over there should not have cost him his job. Later, I went on the 2005 Lions tour [to New Zealand] and spoke to a number of the Irish guys. Nearly all of the players got on well with Warren. In fact, a lot of them spoke very highly of him, although I do not think Keith Wood [the Ireland captain in 2001] and he were exactly a match made in heaven. Given Keith's standing in Ireland, that was perhaps a slight problem, but it all remains a bit of a mystery.

Wasps defeated Munster 37–32 in an epic tie. Dallaglio wrote:

> After the game, I gave Warren a bit of a hug, and, for a guy who normally has a slight poker face, it was strange to see a permanent smile that evening. He had returned to Ireland and, without saying a word, had made his point. He told them everything he needed to, which is that they had made the wrong decision. They never discovered the more that he had to give. Their loss was our gain.

The Welsh Rugby Union complained to BBC Wales about the Gatland feature. The coach was concerned that an important match for Wales was being turned into a personality clash. When he announced his team for Croke Park on the Tuesday before the game, he was not asked directly about O'Sullivan, merely how he felt about going back to Ireland. 'They have some experienced campaigners who were young guys starting out when I was in charge of Ireland,' he said. 'It has been nice to watch their progress and see how well they have done. I am looking forward to catching up with a few of them afterwards. I have a number of friends in Ireland and might have a pint of Guinness with them afterwards. If things had not turned out as they did in 2001, I would not have had the chance to go to Wasps. My ambition had been to take Ireland to the 2003 World Cup and then go back to New Zealand. It is strange how things turn out. I finished with Ireland and had eight job offers within a couple of weeks. One was from Wasps, and going there was a great decision. I am happy with the way my rugby path has gone. I have still yet to apply for a job, and that is quite a nice position to be in. What happened with Ireland was a long time ago, and I have been back to Lansdowne Road since. I got everything out of my system then. Saturday is about the Wales team, not me.'

Earlier, speaking on BBC Wales, he had praised O'Sullivan, saying, 'Ireland have done well under Eddie, winning a couple of Triple Crowns. They will be disappointed with the World Cup, but they have bounced back and are one of the most experienced sides in world rugby. My experiences in Ireland were fantastic; I had a brilliant time there. What happened at the end was disappointing, but I can hold my head high when I think about what I did for Irish rugby. I think I made a difference and having been involved when we won nine of our last eleven games with me in charge, it was the decision of a few individuals to say thanks for what I had done for Ireland. It was disappointing, but I am a great believer in what will be, will be.'

O'Sullivan was also asked by the media to cast his mind back seven years, but he had other issues to wrestle with. Even though he had a four-year contract, he was under pressure after a poor World Cup campaign and a flat start to the Six Nations, which an ultimately convincing victory over Scotland had done little to alleviate. If Gatland had had cause to feel hard done by in 2001, Ireland had prospered under O'Sullivan, winning three Triple Crowns out of four after the 2003 World Cup, and they had only lost one of their previous twelve Six Nations matches against fellow home union sides, against Wales in 2005. Yet they had never managed to take the final step and secure the Grand Slam by defeating France. Wales's 2005 success hurt O'Sullivan because it had come out of nowhere, and there was a feeling in 2007, when France snatched victory at Croke Park with a last-minute try to deny Ireland once more, that O'Sullivan's team had reached the summit and was starting its descent. The last thing he needed was a ghost from the past in the form of Gatland coming back to haunt him. 'It is a Six Nations match between Ireland and Wales, and Warren and I have to coach the teams,' he said. 'It makes great lines for you guys in the media, but it would be foolish for us to get wrapped up in it all. The relationship between Warren and me is fine. We will both be focusing on our jobs.'

Gatland used the media to wind up O'Sullivan and his team. He said he would be posting up in the players' room a comment by the Ireland hooker Rory Best that Wales might have won three matches but they had yet to meet decent opposition, while he claimed that the Ireland captain Brian O'Driscoll had lost a yard of pace. O'Sullivan bit, saying on the eve of the match, 'You can drum up what was said into something more, but Rory knows the landscape tomorrow better than anybody. What Wales are doing might have been great in the amateur days, but I think we have moved beyond ra-ra-ra. We are talking about professional players who prepare meticulously for a game. Some throwaway comment is not going to be the hinge on which you win a match. That is a very dated view on how teams prepare to play. We have all moved on.' But the moving on was to come.

Gatland made four changes to the team that had beaten Italy. Mike Phillips replaced Dwayne Peel, Huw Bennett and Adam Jones came back into the front row, although Bennett was to pull out on the eve of the match after going down with a virus, and Alun Wyn Jones came back into the second row after recovering from his ankle injury. It meant that Stephen Jones retained his position at outside-half ahead of James Hook; this was the topic that dominated the questioning at the team announcement, much to the despair of Gatland, who lamented that the Welsh had an unhealthy obsession with the outside-half position. That did not stop him from then launching into a peroration on the virtues of the Ireland fly-half Ronan O'Gara, a player first capped when Gatland was in charge of Ireland. 'When he is on form, he is their key,' said Gatland. 'He controls their game in attack and defence, and we will have to stop him. We have to put him under pressure and make him make a few tackles.'

The fact that the debate over Hook and Stephen Jones was materially different to the previous year, when Hook had played at inside-centre and there was a clamour for him to be given the number 10 jersey, contributed to a meaningful competition between the two players. Wales went into the Ireland game having landed twenty-one kicks at goal out of twenty-one in the Six Nations, Hook supplying eleven and Jones ten. It was far removed from the World Cup match against Fiji when Hook missed a penalty from in front of the posts and Jones hit the upright with a late conversion. 'I was hoping no one would pick up on the fact that we had not missed a goal-kick yet,' said the Wales kicking coach Neil Jenkins, whose record tally of 1,090 international points was to be broken by Jonny Wilkinson a few hours after Wales had played at Croke Park. 'People forget that Fiji was the exception rather than the rule. Before the World Cup, we had missed 18 kicks in 17 internationals, and the players have all put a lot of work in. There are going to be days when you miss kicks you would normally be expected to land – I had them as a player. James missed a sitter against Fiji, but I remember Jonny Wilkinson fluffing quite an easy one for England against Wales at Wembley in 1999. It will be a test for the kickers, because we have never played at Croke Park before. One quarter of the ground is open, and that will make the wind swirl.'

Gavin Henson had yet to be asked to take a kick, not least because of an Achilles tendon injury he had been carrying during the tournament. It also restricted his kicking out of hand, although he was to launch one 65-yarder into the wind at Croke Park after winning a crucial turnover. Henson had had a quiet tournament media wise, but he had been influential on the field, revelling in the responsibility given to him by Shaun Edwards. The way Gatland had changed the side after every victory and the impact made by the new management team had kept the spotlight off Henson, but it shone on him at the start of the week of the Ireland game after he had appeared on *Scrum V*. The hook to the interview was the last time Wales had played in Dublin in 2006, the first match after Mike Ruddock had departed as head coach, Henson had been restored to the squad for the first time since the publication of his autobiography, and it was probably no coincidence that the captain Gareth Thomas had been ruled out for the rest of that season because of illness. Henson found himself on the field after just 20 minutes, replacing the outside-half Stephen Jones, who had suffered a dead leg. He was given a hostile reception by the crowd after having criticised the Ireland captain Brian O'Driscoll in his book, and while Wales had been leading when Jones went off, they slumped to a heavy defeat. Henson, playing in an unfamiliar position and having had little time to acquaint himself with a new set of moves, said afterwards that he felt suicidal.

As he reflected on the past on *Scrum V*, he started to compare it with the present, hitting the next day's headlines in the process. 'There is a different approach under the coaches we have now,' he said. 'They are pretty strict, and they command respect. We are all living on the edge. Everyone knows that they are one bad training session away from not being picked. We had a poor session the other day, and Warren Gatland was speaking his mind at lunch, saying that perhaps he should change the side. It means people are working as hard as they can. Everyone can see who the coaches are and who the players are. Before, we had senior players who would voice-up a lot, and you did not know whether to listen to them or the coaches. Sometimes, the senior players would overrule the coaches, and it did not quite work, I felt. It has totally turned around now: you know where you stand with these coaches, and that is when players react the best. I feel I am learning every day, and what a player wants from a coach is to be taught new things and to be shown a way of playing that inspires you. It has been refreshing, totally different to what I have experienced under other coaches. None of us can feel comfortable that we will be in the side to face Ireland, and everyone is striving hard to make the starting line-up.'

There was still a forum for senior players to air their views, and Gatland would ask for advice when he felt it was necessary. Unsolicited suggestions, which had been a feature of previous regimes, were discouraged. When Mike Ruddock took over as the Wales head coach in 2004 and brought Clive Griffiths in as defence coach, they wanted to introduce a blitz defence. Some senior players at the time said that it would not work at international level, and the plan was dropped. Ruddock's successor, Gareth Jenkins, also favoured the blitz, but he too met with resistance. The answer of Gatland and Edwards was to pick thirteen Ospreys, and it might have been fifteen but for the fact that the two positions at Twickenham that were not filled by Ospreys were because the region fielded non-Welsh players in them. Gatland and Edwards's message was simple: no blitz, no place. No debate: the system did work at international level, with Wales conceding just two tries in their five matches.

There would be no comeback on Henson from his peers, because player power was now defined not by how they flexed their muscles off the field, but by the arm-wrestles they undertook on it. If Wales had thrived on avoiding contact in 2005, they were now engaged in a power game. The second row Ian Gough revealed that he had lost 11 lb during the victory over Italy after hitting more than 40 rucks. 'I was absolutely exhausted at the end,' he said. 'We are pushed hard in training by the coaches, and that is how we are playing. Shaun Edwards will bite your leg off in training if you miss a tackle, and his tenacity and enthusiasm rub off on you. No one wants to upset him. A few boys have had a tongue-lashing, but I have managed to avoid one so far. He has made a huge difference to us, and I have nothing but total admiration for the man.'

Gough was one of only three players in the Wales squad who had enjoyed success against Ireland in Dublin. Along with Stephen Jones and Shane Williams, he started the 23–19 victory at Lansdowne Road in 2000, a match that saw Gatland in charge of Ireland and up against another New Zealander, Graham Henry. Gough was now involved in his eighth championship, having made his first appearance in it against Scotland in 1999, but only once, in 2006, had he started every match. After appearing against Scotland in 2002, he had to wait another four years for his next Six Nations start, having played a bit-part role in the 2005 Grand Slam success as a replacement against Italy. Gough was to lead the side out against France in 2008 to mark his 50th cap, ten years after he had been awarded his first against South Africa, and he embodied the difference between Gatland's Wales and the Wales of the Scott Johnson and Mike Ruddock era: undemonstrative with a strong work ethic, he tackled far more than he handled. He brought old-fashioned qualities to the second row – not for nothing did the two lock positions become known as the boiler house – and, in his own selfless way, his indefatigability contributed as much to the success in 2008 as the tries of Shane Williams.

'We know we are going to have to put in our most complete performance of the championship if we are going to beat Ireland,' he said. 'We have not put in a full 80 minutes yet: we were outplayed in the first half against England, and it took us 50 minutes to break down Italy. Ireland are a strong, physical side who can mix it with anyone. They are very good at what they do, and in Ronan O'Gara they have a very clever outside-half. We do not have a great recent record in Dublin, but we had a far worse one at Twickenham a few weeks ago. We know we are going to have to go up a gear, but we also know that we are capable of doing that. We know exactly how hard we are going to have to work, and I suspect I will be losing a few more pounds this weekend.'

Gough's second-row partner was the fit again Alun Wyn Jones. They were up against the experienced Ireland pairing of Donncha O'Callaghan and Paul O'Connell, the 2005 Lion who had missed the start of the Six Nations through injury, returning as a replacement against Scotland. 'They have got a very strong partnership, a sweet-and-sour combination, if you like,' said Jones. 'O'Connell is a talisman who grafts and acts like an extra back rower, while O'Callaghan backs him up with an extra work ethic. Ireland are an experienced side in general, and we are going to need to be disciplined, but we will be prepared. People have been going on about the toughness of the new coaching team. They are hard taskmasters, but we have not been crawling under any barbed wire or carrying any flaming logs. It's been taxing, very taxing, but you only get out what you put in. We have been taken out of our comfort zone, which is what we needed. We have always had the confidence and the ability to win, but we have usually come up short. That has changed, and the approach being taken by the coaches suits the players we have.'

After the Ireland match, Shaun Edwards struggled to find praise high enough for Shane Williams, but his priority was to give credit to Wales's front five; back in 2005, Wales were widely accused of doing well despite deficiencies up front. 'Supporters have to realise how hard the tight-five forwards have worked,' said Edwards. 'They are really putting their bodies through distress, and what they are doing really hurts. That is one of the reasons why we have been winning games. The forwards are suffering for the nation, but they are heroes and should be lauded for their Herculean efforts. They have been receptive to new ideas, and they carry out what you ask of them to the letter. I have been humbled by the amount of respect they have shown me.'

Ireland were forced to make a late reshuffle when Geordan Murphy and Girvan Dempsey both failed fitness tests on the Thursday. O'Sullivan had kept the full-back position open in the hope that one of them would be passed fit, but he had to move the 21-year-old Rob Kearney from the wing, with Shane Horgan being promoted from the bench. A feature of O'Sullivan's seven-year reign had been his loyalty to players, but Horgan was no longer a regular starter, the scrum-half Peter Stringer had been dropped to the bench during the World Cup, where he remained for the entire Six Nations campaign, while the flanker Simon Easterby, the Llanelli Scarlets captain, had lost his place in the starting line-up after the opening weekend victory over Italy. Yet despite Wales's strong start to the championship and Ireland's struggle for momentum, it was generally regarded as a 50–50 encounter. The former Ireland full-back Conor O'Shea, who was the then head of the national academy in England, articulated the thoughts of more than a few when he wrote on the RTE website that while he thought Wales could win, he did not expect them to:

> How could a team which lost in the World Cup to Fiji have turned things round so spectacularly? First and foremost, they have talent. Second, they recruited a winner in Warren Gatland. When you examine the Welsh claim to be back at their best, you look at

their matches to date and you know they are a long way off. They looked like they could be on the end of a pasting at Twickenham, but they hung in there, and as England imploded in the second half they showed one of their great traits: the ability to take half a chance when given it. In the next two games, they were under the cosh, but in both they showed enough grit and opportunism to win comfortably. Where does this never-say-die attitude come from? Look up from the pitch and to the stand, and look at Warren Gatland and his sidekick Shaun Edwards and you have the answer.

Gats took over as Ireland coach in 1998, when I was still involved, and at 34 was more like a player–coach. He was close to the team and knew what made individual players tick, but he was different in that he preached loyalty to the group and also showed it. A lot of coaches talk about loyalty but, when the pressure comes on, they don't show it. Gats is different. You know that if you give him everything, he will give it back to you in spades. That is a massive thing for a player. One of Warren's other great traits is his security as a person. He has no problems seeing where others can help and allowing that person their head within his team to deliver what he can't. Through the years with Wasps, he let Craig White, his conditioner from his Ireland days, set the physical training programme. He allowed Shaun Edwards to do most of the coaching and also let senior players such as Lawrence Dallaglio rule the roost in terms of player empowerment. A lot of chiefs, you might think, but don't be under any illusions: everyone knew who was boss and where the buck stopped. Gats was the man. For all the excitement we should see on the pitch on Saturday, it will be the winning coach that I look forward to watching. They will both pretend it means nothing, but deep down this is more than just another match. It is two outstanding coaches who finally get to face off. A classic beckons.

It proved more of a classic than the last occasion Wales had gone to Dublin on the trail of the Triple Crown. That was back in 1988 after opening victories at Twickenham and against Scotland in Cardiff had been achieved in some style, but Lansdowne Road saw a tight, error-ridden, forward-orientated contest shaded by Wales 12–9. Gatland would have taken the same score after the ugliest 80 minutes ever witnessed, but his team were to go one point better in terms of margin of victory. A swirling wind greeted the players, and Ireland gave Wales first use of the breeze. Wales were unable to use the wind advantage initially as Ireland piled into them, driving down narrow channels through their forwards, not wanting to get drawn into a fast, open game on the one hand and intent on soaking up the time Wales had the wind at their backs. O'Gara kicked a penalty under the posts before Neil Jenkins's fear that advertising the fact Hook and Stephen Jones had not missed a kick between them would tempt fate became reality when Jones, from a comfortable distance, screwed his kick wide. O'Gara kicked a second penalty before Mike Phillips, not for the last time in the half, made a telling contribution. Ireland had struggled to create, despite enjoying the bulk of possession, but a mazy run by Horgan took him within sight of the Wales line. The wing tried to outpace Phillips, but the scrum-half kept up and used his strength not just to tackle Horgan, but to check his momentum. As Horgan felt himself falling, he reached out and extended his right arm for the line, but the ball was grounded inches short. Phillips showed how hard was Wales's new resolve, how much further they were prepared to go for Gatland and Edwards. His strength and technique saved Wales from going 13 points down. Match-winning is not the preserve of try scorers.

Phillips's next significant moment will not take up as much room in his scrapbook. Wales had pulled back to 6–3 behind through a Stephen Jones penalty when, in stoppage time at the end of the first period, the Ireland prop Marcus Horan killed the ball at a ruck under his own posts. The English referee Wayne Barnes blew for a penalty, but Phillips added a punishment of his own by dropping his knee on Horan's ribs. The penalty was reversed, costing Wales three points, and Phillips was given ten minutes in the sin-bin, leaving Wales a man down and needing Shane Williams to fill in at scrum-half. 'I wanted to shoot myself,' said Phillips afterwards. 'But I thought Horan was making a meal of it. I was just trying to get the ball off him, and I hardly touched him really. It perhaps looked a bit worse than it was. Half-time was a bit uncomfortable for me. I apologised to the players, and they really dug deep while I was off the field. The fact we came through that period without conceding was a big factor in the match.' The concern for Phillips would be whether Gatland held the act of indiscipline against him and left him out of the Grand Slam match against France. 'I did think about not bringing Mike back on when his ten minutes were up and substituting him,' said Gatland, 'but he had made a try-saving tackle, and we gave him another chance.'

Wales equalised when Phillips was in the sin-bin through a second Jones penalty, and Shane Williams was enjoying the return to scrum-half, the position he occupied when he joined Neath at the end of the 1990s only to find himself very quickly converted to the wing. 'You forget how hard it is in the position and how involved you get,' he said afterwards. 'The game revolves around you, and I enjoyed it, but only for ten minutes. I could shout at the forwards and call them names, but I was glad to give the job back to Mike.' Williams had gone to the 2003 World Cup with Wales as third-choice scrum-half, only to prove during the tournament that he was a wing. And it was Williams, with his fifth try of the tournament, who provided the game's decisive moment. Martyn Williams dispossessed Kearney, and Stephen Jones moved right, taking out a defender with a sweetly timed pass to Shane Williams. The wing had it all to do, with Ireland not short of covering defenders, but he managed to put a judder in the centre Andrew Trimble's step with a subtle change of pace and then saw him off with a hand-off. Pace and strength did the rest as the left-wing touched down in the right-hand corner to equal Gareth Thomas's record of 40 tries for Wales. 'I am not the kind of winger who sits on the touchline having a cup of tea until the ball comes my way. If that means I have to score tries on the right while playing on the left, I will do it.' And then, in a moment of prescience given what was to happen a week later, he added, 'I have scored a couple on the right-hand side this Six Nations and a couple on the left, so I am due one under the posts now.'

Jones converted Williams's try to put Wales 13–6 ahead. They were keeping the ball for long periods and playing as if they were at the Millennium Stadium. Ryan Jones was leading by example at number 8 and showing that Gatland had been inspired to award him the captaincy. There were more experienced contenders the coach could have turned to, and the easy option would have been to say that Jones needed time to feel his way back into the side after his time out with injury, but he had two advantages: he was the captain of the Ospreys, the region Wales were drawing most heavily from, and although he had been a member of the 2005 Grand Slam side, he had not been part of the squad under Steve Hansen and Scott Johnson between 2002 and 2004. He had won his first cap under Ruddock and was out of the side in 2006 when the Ruddock affair blew up. His appointment did not bind Gatland in any way to the past and was part of the process of moving forward.

Wales were producing their best rugby of the tournament in terms of organisation and control. If some people had expected their forwards to struggle, it was Ireland who were blowing. They had threatened only fitfully, and their best attack in the third quarter ended when Henson, who had earlier stopped Horgan with a shuddering tackle, won a turnover and kicked the ball 65 yards into touch into the wind. As it galvanised Wales, so it deflated Ireland, who minutes later conceded the game's only try. Wales looked in total control when Ireland launched their next meaningful attack. Eoin Reddan, Edwards's scrum-half at Wasps, fed his number 8, James Heaslip, and looped around the forward to await a potential try-scoring pass. Martyn Williams was alert to the danger but realising he could not catch Reddan stuck out a foot and tripped him up. The referee was up with play and saw what had happened. Williams received a yellow card, and O'Gara then kicked two penalties to bring his side back to within a point. However, Wales's defence again held firm, despite operating under the handicap of being not just a man down but being without one of their two defence captains.

Wales again kicked to touch as a last resort and only gave Ireland two lineouts. It meant the ball-in-play time was again high, and Wales dominated in terms of territory and possession. But they never escaped on the scoreboard, and, as the match entered its final six minutes, one mistake would decide it.

Enter Ireland's replacement hooker, Bernard Jackman. Spotting Ryan Jones hanging out of a ruck on his knees on Ireland's ten-yard line, Jackman thumped into the Wales captain and committed two offences in one: he entered the breakdown from the side and he took out a player off the ball in an act of stupidity born of frustration. It should have merited a yellow card, and Jones was to leave the field injured, but Wales had to be content with three points from the boot of Hook, who ten minutes before had come on as a replacement for Jones. Wales led 16–12, and, with time ticking away, Ireland effectively had to score a try to maintain their remarkable recent record against Wales of losing just five times in twenty-one internationals. They never had a chance: Wales, as they had done in the closing minutes at Twickenham, played keep ball. O'Driscoll had left the field with a hamstring injury, and Gatland, like Ruddock, was on course for a Grand Slam in his first season in charge of Wales.

'It is in our hands now,' he said after showing real emotion for the first time following a victory. 'We are in control of our own destiny, and that is all you can ask at this stage of the campaign. I still believe we are up to a couple of years away from being a pretty good side, but we are continuing to make progress. There are still areas to work on: we had opportunities to put the game beyond Ireland and we did not take them, while we put ourselves under pressure with two yellow cards. I can't say I was happy at half-time, but the players dug deep.' Gatland had a final say about the O'Sullivan issue. 'It was not about me and Eddie,' he said. 'That was a side issue, and what mattered was Wales playing Ireland. I thought the whole Eddie O'Sullivan thing was over the top. I respect him, and he has been very professional in some of the things he has said. Perhaps I could learn something from that myself.'

Ryan Jones was presented with the Triple Crown trophy, which had been won by Ireland three times and Wales twice since the 2003 World Cup. 'You earn your rewards,' he said. 'You cannot put moments like this into words, but we want to go one better and claim the Grand Slam. The hype in Wales in the build-up to the France game next Saturday is going to be almost unbearable. I will be keeping my head down, shutting the curtains and locking the door. And I will turn my answer phone off. We know we cannot get caught up in all of that. We have to keep working hard, and what was pleasing for me was the way we closed the games out against both England and Ireland. We showed maturity and composure, and, for me, that is far more impressive than seeing us run in tries from out wide. We have developed a physical edge, and we will not be bullied by anyone. We can mix it with anyone.'

Stephen Jones was left to reflect on the old saying about roosters and feather dusters. A year before, Wales had gone into their final game of the Six Nations having lost four matches out of four. He was the captain, and there was a clamour for him to be dropped. When he pulled out of the side to face England on the last weekend, conspiracy theorists hypothesised that he had been dropped by the back door, but the haunted look he wore then was replaced by a large grin as he anticipated another tilt at a Grand Slam. 'Last year was very difficult, and to bounce back in the way we have is testament to the character and dedication of the players,' he said. 'From the moment he came in, Warren Gatland told us that he expected us to work hard. He puts you under pressure and keeps you thinking all the time, and it has created a healthy environment. He has demanded a lot from us, and we showed how far we have come by producing a huge victory in a city where we have struggled in recent years.'

Wales were on the trail of their tenth Grand Slam. They were the first country to achieve the feat, exactly 100 years before, although in those days France were not members of the Five Nations and played friendlies against the home unions before joining the championship in 1910. Wales had secured their first Slam by defeating Ireland 11–5 in Belfast on 14 March. A century on and they were facing France on 15 March. And there was a greater coincidence. The day after Wales defeated Ireland, Cardiff City won 2–0 at Middlesbrough to make their first FA Cup semi-final for 81 years. With Chelsea and Manchester United also losing in the last eight, it meant that only one club from the top flight would be represented in the semi-finals. The year that had last happened? 1908.

8

THE THREE WS

The future enters into us, in order to transform us,
long before it happens.

Rainer Maria Wilke

18 MAY 1988. IF, OR WHEN, WARREN GATLAND GETS
around to writing his autobiography, one chapter
title should be 'Wales – My Part in Their Downfall'. Wales
are in Hamilton at the start of the New Zealand winter,
playing Waikato in the first of eight matches on a tour
they had not made for nineteen years. They had won the
Triple Crown in the 1988 Five Nations, finishing joint top
of the table with France; they would have been outright
champions had today's system of separating teams by using
points difference been in force then. In April, their coach
Tony Gray had been voted the European coach of the
year. Under him, Wales had started to play with a swagger

again and were blessed with an array of attacking backs in Jonathan Davies, Mark Ring, Bleddyn Bowen, John Devereux, Adrian Hadley and Ieuan Evans, well prompted by Robert Jones at scrum-half. If they did not possess the most fearsome pack, they had in the second row Robert Norster arguably the best lineout forward in the world game. They travelled to the land of the long white cloud armed with a not insignificant element of hope, even if expectation was tempered by the fact that the previous year New Zealand had beaten Wales 49–6 in the World Cup semi-final en route to lifting the Webb Ellis Trophy. They were, by some margin, the leading team in the world, while Wales were flying the European banner. 'We have to go out there with the assumption that we are going to win matches,' said Gray before the squad departed for Auckland. 'We have developed sufficiently in the last few months to make the experience of the World Cup work to our advantage. The best is still to come of this side.'

Waikato lay in wait first. Although they were ranked the sixth strongest of New Zealand's provinces, they had a reputation for unsettling touring sides. They were to New Zealand what Pontypool and Neath were then to Wales and Gloucester to England: unfashionable but with a strong sense of community. One writer compared the prospect of playing Waikato in Hamilton to walking barefoot on a pavement on a frosty morning or running into an electric fence clad merely in shorts. They had defeated France 18–15 in 1979 and in 1986 drew 21–21 with Australia, who were then regarded as New Zealand's greatest threat in the inaugural World Cup. In 1990, they were to defeat the Wallabies 21–10.

Wales brought the rain with them to Hamilton; it poured

virtually non-stop for the week they were in the town after arriving from Heathrow, somewhat fittingly, as '*waikato*' is the Maori word for flowing water, although the downpour stopped just before the start of the game at Rugby Park. The real deluge was to come. It was a region known for its farmland, and the Waikato team's mascot was a pantomime cow called Mooloo, reflecting the importance of the dairy industry to the region. Each shop in the town centre seemed to have its own Mooloo in the build-up to the Wales game, making walking down the main street hazardous, as the plastic cows were, by virtue of their size, generally parked outside. It was an apposite symbol given what Wales were to be served up, a steak 'ta-ta', as it were.

Gatland was then 24 and in his third season as Waikato's hooker, having until the age of 21 played at number 8. Along with his two props, Richard Loe and Graham Purvis, he was selected for New Zealand's 1989 tour to Wales and Ireland. Gatland and Purvis sat on the bench for both matches, while Loe played in each at tight-head prop. When Gatland finished at Waikato in 1994, he had played a then record 140 matches for the side. Before the Wales match in 1988, he had impressed in a New Zealand trial and that, together with his display against Wales, earned him a place in the All Blacks' squad that went on a three-Test tour to Australia later that year. He remained in the squad for four years and played seventeen matches for the All Blacks without ever winning a cap. Sean Fitzpatrick, three months his junior, stood in his way, and Gatland never left the bench in an era when clotting the end of matches with a raft of replacements was regarded as cheapening the value of a cap and when it was rare for anyone to come on other than in the case of injury, and Fitzpatrick, like

Shaun Edwards, did not do injured. In 1992, he led a New Zealand XV in two matches against England B, having taken over the Waikato captaincy in the middle of 1988. Gatland started his coaching career in 1989 with Taupiri, a club in the north of Waikato with the same coloured strip as Wasps. He became the player–coach at Galwegians the following year, having shown on the All Blacks' tour to Australia in 1988 an originality of thought. He introduced a new theme to warm-up sessions before training, a hybrid game incorporating chunks of Australian Rules Football and Gaelic Football, something that proved popular with the players.

The Waikato team contained other players who were to move abroad, notably the second row John Mitchell, who coached in Ireland and became Clive Woodward's assistant at England before taking charge of New Zealand. Waikato had an imposing pack of forwards, and while Wales took an early 7–0 lead before a capacity thirty-thousand crowd, they were gradually worn down and lost 28–19, with Loe scoring two of his side's four tries. The Triple Crown seemed another world away. 'They fell flat on their faces,' said the Waikato coach Duncan Dysart afterwards. 'If you are going to compete in New Zealand, you have to get your forwards moving around the paddock.' A Welsh journalist had provided Dysart with a video of one of Wales's Five Nations matches. 'It was invaluable,' said the coach. 'We deduced a tremendous amount from studying their play. We saw that they packed high in the rucks and mauls and that only one of their loose forwards got around the paddock. We made sure we drove in low, and we split them repeatedly. We also took them in the scrum.' A bunch of leeks had been placed on the halfway line before the kick-off. By the time the players ran out, the symbols of Welshness had wilted.

And it got worse. Wales lost to Wellington before defeating Otago in the week of the first Test against the All Blacks in Christchurch. It was an even more one-sided contest than the previous year's World Cup semi-final. Wales lost 52–3, and although they enjoyed a romp against Hawkes Bay, a draw at Taranaki and a 27–9 defeat to North Auckland in Whangerei, where one spectator stood up after slapstick defending had cost Wales another try, pulled a bugle out of his jacket and sounded the last post. New Zealand won the second Test; in three internationals, they had plundered Wales for one hundred and fifty-five points. In one sense, the appointment of Gatland as the Wales head coach in 2007 brought a sense of closure. The defeat to Waikato was the start of a spiral of steep decline to which the Welsh Rugby Union responded by sacking coaches after every unbearable indignity. Gray was the first to go, a month after returning from New Zealand. The WRU not only overlooked his achievements before the tour, but failed to consider just how far the domestic game in New Zealand had moved ahead of Welsh club rugby. It was a knee-jerk reaction, and the average survival period of a coach between that time and Gatland's arrival was less than two years.

Wales quickly had a chance of revenge with New Zealand touring in the autumn of 1989 on a seven-match visit that took in Cardiff, Pontypool, Swansea, Neath, Llanelli and Newport before the international at the National Stadium. Gatland played in two of the games, against Swansea and Newport, with Fitzpatrick occupying the hooker's jersey the rest of the time. Gatland scored the All Blacks' first try at Swansea, while at Rodney

Parade against easily the weakest of the sides they faced that trip, he and his teammates had to chase after the Newport players to perform the pre-match haka because the home team decided to form a huddle under their own posts rather than face up to the war chant. The Test was again one-sided, with the All Blacks winning 34–9, their best result in Cardiff. It was the fifth successive match between the sides that New Zealand had created a record in victory. Wales fielded two players who were to be in charge of regional sides when Gatland came to work in Wales in 2007, David Young (Cardiff Blues) and Phil Davies (Llanelli Scarlets). The Wales coach John Ryan, Gray's successor, had three months left in the post.

The second leg of the trip was to Ireland. Gatland played in the 36–9 victory over Leinster and in the 40–6 success over Connacht. He was on the bench for the international against Ireland at Lansdowne Road, which the All Blacks won 23–6, but played no part in the final match of the visit, against the Barbarians at Twickenham. Earlier in the tour, the New Zealand prop Craig Dowd (who was later to team up with Gatland at Wasps) had been in London shopping when the then chairman of Galwegians, Michael Heaslip, recognised him and bustled over. Heaslip said he was looking for a coach and would any of the All Blacks be interested. Dowd said to leave it with him, and when New Zealand arrived in Galway to prepare for the match against Connacht, Heaslip sought him out. Dowd introduced Gatland, and he hit it off immediately with Heaslip and the chairman's brother Danno, who by 2008 had become the president of Galwegians, agreeing to return before the start of the 1990–91 season when he would be player–coach. It was the amateur era, and it meant that Gatland and his wife Trudy would have to leave their teaching jobs in New Zealand and find positions in Ireland.

'We had decided as a club that we needed to change direction,' said Danno Heaslip. 'New Zealand were the best team in the world, and it made sense to see if any of the All Blacks would be interested in coming over. We met Warren, and we could not have made a better choice. We were struggling for players, and things were, quite frankly, falling down. I remember his first game vividly: we were playing in Sligo, which was some eighty-five miles away, and we had still not left the clubhouse even though there were less than three hours to go before kick-off. Warren ordered everyone to get on the bus and told the driver to put the thing in gear and take off, even though one of the players was still in the toilet and a couple of stragglers were yet to show up. He said they would have to make their own way. We were a few miles from the ground when he told the driver to pull over. He then told all the players to get out. There they were, standing around in their ordinary clothes and shoes, when Warren shouts at the driver to move on, barking at the squad to run behind the coach. He made them do that for a mile or so before letting them back on. He showed them straight away who the boss was and that he would not tolerate any slacking.

'He was strict, but he was not a bully. His attitude was that if you were not prepared to do it his way, you went somewhere else. It was not long before we went on a 13-match winning run. That was unheard of, absolutely incredible. Whereas before we were struggling for numbers, now we had players knocking down the door. We ended up having to turn some away. They were coming from everywhere, and it was all down to Warren. I guess we were breaking the mould by having a New Zealander coaching the club. The All Blacks had an aura about them, and to be coached by one of them was something everyone seemed to want on their CV. He not only transformed our club, but rugby in the west of Ireland. I made a friend for life, and I really envy people in Wales now, because not only have they got one of the best coaches in the world, but they have a genuinely nice guy. Warren is superb with people. He believes in working hard, getting the job done and then having a bit of relaxation time.'

The Gatlands spent four years shuttling between Galway and Waikato, Galwegians winning two Connacht League titles and being promoted to the All Ireland League in 1992, before tragedy struck and their baby daughter Shauna died. The Heaslips insisted that they return to New Zealand immediately. 'That gesture stayed with Warren Gatland,' wrote the journalist Brendan Fanning in his book on Irish rugby in the professional era, *From There to Here*. 'A club that had invested heavily in him was prepared to put it aside so that he could sort himself out at home. He did not know it then, but he would be back.'

Gatland had returned to teaching in Waikato and had been taken on as a coach by Thames Valley when, in 1996, he received a telephone call from Connacht. They were looking for a new coach after failing to agree terms with Eddie O'Sullivan, and they were shortly to leave for a pre-season tour of Sweden. It would also mean taking over from O'Sullivan at Galwegians, because, in the early days of professionalism, there were no full-time posts in Irish provincial rugby and jobs were combined. Gatland found himself dropping everything and finding out the times of flights from Auckland to Stockholm. 'I'd never been to Sweden,' he said looking back at times past in 2008. 'That was it. I said yes.' It would not be long before he and O'Sullivan crossed paths again.

'Eddie O'Sullivan was looking for a three-year contract from Connacht, but he was only offered twelve months, and the talks broke down,' said Fanning. 'He had taken over from Gatland at Galwegians, and I think he felt that Connacht would come back from their tour, say that a terrible mistake had been made and agree terms with him. The speed with which Connacht acted surprised everyone, and when Gatland was let go by Ireland in 2001 to be replaced by O'Sullivan, it did have a context.'

A theme was starting to emerge in Gatland's rugby career. He had played for a province that was not regarded as being among New Zealand's establishment elite, although they were the provincial champions when they humbled the 1993 Lions 38–10, a match in which the hooker scored the last of his side's five tries, and his first two coaching jobs had come at sides that were struggling. Connacht was the runt of the Irish provincial litter, a distinct fourth behind Munster, Leinster and Ulster. The Irish Rugby Football Union was to provoke a storm of protest the following decade when it announced a plan to strip Connacht of its central funding, hastily backing down. In the early days of the Celtic League in the 2000s, Ulster, Munster and Leinster were guaranteed Heineken Cup places no matter whether Connacht finished above them in the table. When Gatland took over as the Wales head coach, one of his reasons for taking the job was that after being knocked out of the World Cup early and slumping to tenth in the world rankings, the only way to go was up. It was pretty much the same when he became Ireland's coach, initially in a caretaker capacity, in the middle of the 1998 Five Nations, and he became Wasps' director of rugby when they were at the bottom of the English Premiership. He has been about giving underdogs bite.

'The strange thing about Wasps,' Gatland said in an interview with *The Independent* in 2004, 'is that they remind me so much of Waikato. There are all these amazing parallels. The Waikato I knew didn't have too many big names – no prima donnas, that's for sure – but had reasonably talented players who got on well and played hard off the field as well as on it. We existed on a work ethic developed over the decades; there was something blue-collar about us, a collective spirit that was pure "us against them". We talked endlessly about the privilege of pulling on the shirt, and when we took the field, our hearts were on our sleeves. You couldn't quantify what we had, and you couldn't buy it, either. I might just as easily be talking about Wasps. People look at Lawrence Dallaglio and Joe Worsley and Rob Howley and say, "Hey, you've got a squad full of stars." But that's not the way it operates here. Lawrence and Joe have just signed new contracts with us – Stuart Abbott and Fraser Waters, too – and they did that because they have a feeling for the club that goes way beyond what they think they can get out of it. It matters to them. Before a big game, we often sit down and talk about honour and togetherness and all the rest of the soppy old bullshit I was familiar with back in Hamilton. It still moves me. I never thought I'd love a team in the way I loved Waikato, but Wasps are special.'

Gatland made an immediate impact with Connacht, and in 1997 they qualified for the knockout stage of the European Conference after defeating Northampton home and away and becoming the first Irish province to win a European match in France when they overcame Bègles-

Bordeaux. He introduced a hard work ethic and made gym sessions competitive. 'You'd be on the bench press and the next thing he would appear over and start leaning on it,' Bernard Jackman, the Connacht hooker at the time, is quoted as saying in Fanning's book – the same Jackman who when Wales played Ireland in the fourth match of their 2008 Grand Slam campaign would concede the penalty six minutes from time which gave Gatland's men a cushion. 'And you would not know when he was going to get off. That was his big thing, and in the first year especially he worked us to the bone. I remember one day early the next season he brought us down to Athlone for a video session, and it was the bluntest couple of hours I think any of us had ever been through. That was the start of professionalism in terms of analysis. He cut right to the bone with a few guys. That was the first place I had heard the term "ruck inspector". After that, we went out on to the field for an hour and "killed" each other. And then we really started to click.'

Gatland was innovative, introducing a 13-man lineout that yielded a few tries for Connacht, and he found himself acting as an adviser to the then Ireland coach, Brian Ashton, the man he was to succeed less than a year later. Another figure who was to go on and coach Wales to a Grand Slam, Mike Ruddock, then in charge at Leinster, was also an adviser to Ashton. 'There was nothing formal, not even any kit,' said Gatland in an interview with *The Observer* in 2008. 'There was no structure surrounding the Ireland set-up. The team's confidence was low.' Ashton had taken over at the start of the 1997 Five Nations, but he left thirteen months later after a one-point defeat to Scotland at Lansdowne Road. He said after it, 'I am not quite sure whose game plan that

159

is, but it has nothing to do with me.' He was struck down by shingles before the next game, against France in Paris, and asked Gatland to take charge of training. Ashton resigned the following week, citing personal reasons, and Gatland was appointed caretaker coach. At 34, he was the youngest head coach in Ireland's history.

If Gatland was to enjoy five victories in his first five matches in charge of Wales, he suffered five defeats in a row with Ireland. France were 33–1 on to win on what would be Ireland's first visit to the Stade de France in 1998. The former Ireland outside-half Tony Ward was in despair. 'Irish rugby has never been more poorly endowed,' he said. 'We have never been so bereft of talent.' As if to prove Ward's point, Gatland produced a shock when he selected the flanker Andy Ward, his fellow New Zealander, to win his first cap – Ward was playing for a third-division club, Ballynahinch. 'Ireland's record in Paris is depressing, but I am trying to eliminate all negative thoughts from the squad,' said Gatland. 'Words like futile have been used about our visit, but if we can be disciplined, creative and get a work ethic going, we can come away with something far higher than the public expects.' Ireland had not won in Paris for twenty-five years, but they were in the lead seven minutes from time, with Ward the man of the match, when the France hooker Raphaël Ibañez was shoved over the line. France were to go on and win the Grand Slam, while Ireland ended up with a whitewash-coated wooden spoon.

Their one heavy defeat was in their final game at Twickenham, 35–17. In the match programme that day, Barry Coughlan wrote:

When he was preparing for his first game against France, he appreciated the mood of discontent that existed amongst Irish rugby supporters. He courted them and pleaded for messages of goodwill to be sent to the team in the build-up to the game. It was not an act of desperation, because the All Blacks had used similar ploys in the past. The squad received 2,000 messages compared to the normal 100–200 for New Zealand.

And then shades of what was to come for Wales a decade later:

> Gatland is confident enough to suggest that the corner will be turned, and he intends to make it difficult for teams to score tries against Ireland in the future. He makes the point that New Zealand, surely the best team in the world, work on defence before they ever think of attack. The bad days are still with Ireland, but Gatland may well be the charismatic figure needed to drag them out of the rut. I have no doubt that he will be offered a contract to lead Ireland into next year's World Cup.

He was. Ireland fared slightly better in the 1999 Five Nations, finishing joint bottom with France after winning one match, against Wales at Wembley. They failed to make the quarter-finals of the World Cup after losing to Argentina in a play-off in Lens. Gatland kept his job, but a consequence was that he was asked to consider appointing Eddie O'Sullivan, who had worked with the United States during the World Cup, as an assistant coach. The IRFU was happy with the progress the forwards had made under Gatland, but felt that the quality of back play was deteriorating. Fanning wrote:

> Eddie O'Sullivan had ambition written in broad capitals across his forehead. Once he was put on the national ticket, one of two things would happen: he would succeed Gatland at some stage, or in time he would move on in search of fulfilment. They weren't going to grow old together. Straight away there was unease: O'Sullivan was hired on a three-year contract, while Gatland was being strung along as if still on probation. His first deal had been for the remainder of the Five Nations in 1998, and the second was up to the end of the 2000 championship. And O'Sullivan walked into a three-year deal to start?

Fanning interviewed Gatland for his book, which was published in 2007:

> 'That was always the frustrating thing,' said the coach. 'You always felt as if you were looking over your back. And that always made it difficult. The decision to appoint another coach after Philip Danaher had left following the World Cup was completely my own. I was asked to meet Eddie. And I did. I spoke to a few people in Connacht, and they advised me against taking him on, but you know . . . I did not have a problem with him coming on board. For me it was always about getting the right person in the job. But I knew there was a bit of baggage.'

Their first match together saw England score fifty points at Twickenham, but Ireland won their next three, including a first win over Scotland for twelve years, their first victory in the championship at Dublin since 1996 and a 27–25 success over France in Paris, a match in which Brian O'Driscoll scored three tries. They finished third in the table on points difference, their best placing since 1987, and the following year were runners-up to England, again on points difference, after winning four of their five games. They ended with a 20–14 victory at Lansdowne Road over England, opponents they had not beaten for seven years. A team that when he took over did not know where its next victory was coming from had won seven Six Nations matches out of nine, but it was not enough to secure him the contract extension through to the 2003 World Cup finals that he sought, with his deal running out at the end of the 2002 championship. His last game in charge was against New Zealand in Dublin in November 2001. Ireland were leading 21–7 in the second half against opponents they had never defeated, only for the All Blacks to rally with three tries in twelve minutes on their way to a 40–29 success.

'The IRFU believed that Gatland had taken Ireland as far as he could,' said Fanning. 'There was a perception of him as a poor planner and that plans for training sessions would be written on the back of scraps of paper which were likely to be torn up at the last minute. He denies this.' Gatland met the IRFU on 26 November to review the year. Two days later, he went to the Berkeley Court Hotel in Dublin to meet union officials. He thought he would be offered a new contract. Instead, he was told that his contract would not be extended, starting immediately.

He was out of a job. As he went out of the hotel's front gate, he saw O'Sullivan driving in. Gatland received a six-figure pay-off. 'Warren was very harshly treated by the IRFU in my view,' said Danno Heaslip. 'Just look at what he has gone on to achieve since. We lost a good man.' Six weeks later, Gatland became Wasps' forwards coach. He had been there little more than a month when, on St David's Day 2002, he took over from Nigel Melville as the club's director of rugby. There were eight league games left, and Wasps were looking down the barrel at relegation. They won six matches in a row. They have won at least one trophy every season since.

In his autobiography, Lawrence Dallaglio wrote:

> Warren had eight or nine job offers in front of him when Ireland mysteriously failed to renew his contract. The fact he chose to come to Wasps had a lot to do with Nigel's promotion of the club to him, and I think it also had something to do with Kiwi pragmatism. Warren looked at our league position, then looked at our list of players, and reckoned there was only one way things could go. After Nigel moved on a short time after Warren had arrived, Warren told the board that they should not feel that they had to give him the rugby director's job. The board had already come to the view that Warren was the man to take the club forward.
>
> Many fundamentals needed to be changed at the club. Facilities and staffing levels at the training ground were two obvious examples. Warren's belief was that unless the facilities were improved and more coaches were employed, the club would not

progress. At one of his early meetings with the board, he produced a list of things he wanted to change, and although none of them was hugely expensive, collectively they added up to quite a bit of money. The board politely said that there was not enough to implement all that he requested. 'OK,' said Warren. 'In that case, I am going to sell Joe Worsley and use whatever transfer fee we get and the money we save in wages to fund the changes I want to make.' Faced with the prospect of losing Joe, one of our best players, the board sharpened up its act and found the funds to help Warren.

Gatland brought in Craig White, who had been part of the Ireland management team under him, as fitness coach and quickly formed a strong working relationship with Shaun Edwards. In Gatland's full three seasons in charge, Wasps won three league titles and two European trophies. To Dallaglio, who had spent his entire senior career at the club, it marked the most glorious chapter in the history of Wasps. Ireland's loss had been Gatland's, and English rugby's, gain, but the pain of rejection was not banished by trophies. 'After Gatland had come back to Ireland with Wasps and beaten Munster in the Heineken Cup semi-final, he came to the after-match media conference,' said Fanning. 'As he sat down, he saw me and, before anyone had asked a question, said he had not liked my comments. The game was played on a Sunday, and I had written in that morning's newspaper, looking back on his departure from Ireland, that he had fallen asleep on the job and that his planning had become poor. Ireland had needed more specialist coaches, especially in defence, but

Gatland learned from what had gone wrong with Ireland. He became more adept at handling the political side, and he became a great leader of management teams. He and Ireland moved on, and, in the end, it was not a bad move for either of them.'

In 2005, Gatland left Wasps and returned to Waikato, where he was appointed head coach. He had been away from New Zealand for nine years, and his last match in charge of Wasps saw them defeat Leicester 39–14 in the Premiership play-off final at Twickenham, the ground to which less than three years later he would travel for his first game back in Britain. He was accused by the media in his first year of making Waikato resemble England. 'I took some criticism for tightening up a few things,' he said in an interview with *The Observer* in 2008. 'There were quite a few people in New Zealand who said that you could not win anything by playing northern-hemisphere style rugby. That criticism pretty much dried up when we won the cup.' (The National Provincial Championship in New Zealand was to be renamed the Air New Zealand Cup.) It was the second time the province had won the tournament; on the previous occasion, in 1992, Gatland was the side's hooker.

If Gatland was to be a contender for the New Zealand job after the 2007 World Cup, he needed to become a Super 12 (soon to become Super 14) head coach. The obvious side was Waikato Chiefs, and in 2006 he became a technical adviser to the franchise, but the head coach Ian Foster signed an extension to his contract that would take him through to 2008. That left Gatland in limbo. Moving to Otago to take charge of the Highlanders did not appeal, and Wales came calling in October 2007 at the right time not just for them, but for Gatland, who two weeks earlier had given up his role with the Chiefs, saying that he wanted to concentrate on his role as Waikato's head coach. 'I was hoping to get an opportunity to be in charge of a Super 14 side, but that hasn't been available to me since I have been back in New Zealand, so you've just got to look at all the chances and opportunities in front of you,' he said at the time to Radio Sport in New Zealand, adding that while his ambition was to take charge of New Zealand, he did not believe he had a chance of succeeding Graham Henry, whose All Blacks side had just been knocked out of the World Cup at the quarter-final stage by France. 'They have not been through that review process, and I presume that they have a number of people ahead of me,' he added.

When Gatland was appointed by Wales, the New Zealand flanker Marty Holah was in his second month with the Ospreys, having joined them from Waikato. 'Warren has got a lot to offer Wales, and he is a guy who will think of more than just the team in terms of rugby,' said Holah. 'He will be concerned about the whole environment, and he will like to have everything controlled around his ways, but that is how most coaches operate these days.' Another wing forward, Simon Easterby, the captain of Llanelli Scarlets, had been given his first Ireland cap by Gatland in 2000. 'He gained a lot of respect from the players,' said Easterby. 'He was very diligent in his preparation, and he will bring a real professionalism to the Wales set-up. I am not surprised that Wales have gone for him when you look at his track record with Wasps and Waikato. He was also the start of Ireland's resurgence, and he created the team we have had for the last six or seven years. He is a quiet man who gets on with his job, and I am sure he already knows a lot about the players he will be working with. He knows the job will carry expectation and that he will have to deliver, but Wales have the right man.'

It was left to Sean Fitzpatrick, the player who had denied his former hooker rival a cap, to chastise the New Zealand Rugby Union for not doing more to keep Gatland. 'I am surprised that New Zealand have let him go so easily,' said Fitzpatrick. 'It is a good move for Wales purely because he is one of the most talented coaches out there.' The former England and Lions second row Paul Ackford, writing in the *Sunday Telegraph*, pointed out:

> Gatland's strength is that he coordinates his people cleverly. His style is inclusive. He is a reliable and canny selector who is not afraid of upsetting people, an aspect which will have endeared him to the Welsh Rugby Union, who have become increasingly disturbed by the player power wielded in the previous regimes of Mike Ruddock and Gareth Jenkins. Gatland will not tolerate such behaviour. He has already displayed his more flinty side to the WRU. When they first contacted him to open negotiations, they had a salary of £180,000 in mind. The figure had risen to around £250,000 by the time the deal had been completed. He could also do with an acknowledgement from the whole of Wales that the job of coaching the Welsh side will only become one of the best jobs in world rugby when everyone – administrators, journalists, players, former players and public – has a realistic sense of precisely where Wales are in the global pecking order. I'll help you here. It's not very high.

Gatland was introduced to the Wales media at the Millennium Stadium on 9 November 2007, nearly 18 years to the day since he had sat on the bench for New Zealand against Wales just a few yards away. 'I know I am Wales's seventh coach in seven years,' he said, 'but when I took charge of Ireland in 1998, I was something like their ninth coach that decade, and I lasted nearly four years. It is not about me coming in, bringing my own back-up team and leaving nothing behind. I want to improve Welsh rugby, and that means working with coaches as well as players. I am confident that I can get Wales climbing up the world rankings. We have a tough start at Twickenham in the Six Nations and people have to be patient, but we will get there.'

So, Gatland swapped one blazer with WRU on it (as in Waikato Rugby Union) for another (as in Welsh Rugby Union). Waikato, Wasps, Wales. The three Ws. Edwards's long association with Wigan made it four. A fifth would constitute a Grand Slam.

9

....

JUST WILLIAMS

The Welsh way is about being prepared
to live off your wits.

Ray Gravell

1 NOVEMBER 2007. PHIL BENNETT, THE OUTSIDE-HALF
and captain when Wales won the Grand Slam in
1978 by defeating France in Cardiff, is standing outside
Stradey Park in Llanelli, the ground where he spent his
entire career in senior rugby. It has been just over a month
since Wales were bundled out of the World Cup. Bennett,
a newspaper columnist and radio pundit, had joined in
the despair after Wales's failure to reach the quarter-finals.
As he huddles in front of the clubhouse in the chill of an
autumn early morning, he reflects: 'Suddenly it does not
seem important any more.'

The day before, 35 years to the day after Llanelli had

defeated the All Blacks at Stradey Park, a match in which Bennett and the recently sacked Wales coach Gareth Jenkins had played, Ray Gravell, the Scarlets' outside-centre that afternoon, had died suddenly at the age of 56 while on holiday in Spain with his family. Gravell had become an iconic figure in Wales, transcending rugby. His funeral at Stradey Park was to attract more than 10,000 mourners. After retiring as a player in 1985, he had worked as an actor and hosted television and radio programmes. He also worked as a touchline reporter for BBC Wales and the Welsh language television station, S4C, playing a match from the sidelines and feeling elation and pain as acutely as any of the players. He had an infectious enthusiasm and, even in Welsh rugby's darkest years, never lost his glow of optimism. 'Have faith,' he would urge after the latest reverse.

Gravell was at the Millennium Stadium in more than spirit when Wales took the field for their final match in the 2008 Six Nations against France. In their final training session the previous day, the Wales squad had worn red T-shirts sporting Gravell's name and the number he wore, 13. His daughters, nine-year-old Gwenan and twelve-year-old Manon, were the mascots for the match day and led the team onto the field. Ian Gough, rather than Ryan Jones, was the first out of the tunnel to mark the occasion of his 50th cap, and his teammates followed several seconds later, marching slowly to a deliberate beat. The England players had walked onto the pitch at Murrayfield the week before, but while they trudged as if taking their final steps before a death sentence was carried out, Wales bore the manner of executioners, steady and unblinking. The emotion of the moment hit Gough as he emerged from the tunnel, but it was only momentary. He took the hands of Gravell's daughters, said a few words to them and waited for his colleagues to join him on their day of destiny.

The roof was closed to keep out the product of a foul March day. Black clouds hovered with the menacing look of Shaun Edwards after his players had let in a soft try. The atmosphere in Cardiff city centre before the final game of the 2005 Six Nations had been frenzied: supporters had waited 27 years for the moment, and Wales in that time had sunk lower than ever before, including the wretched 1920s. Relief mingled with anticipation and the way Wales had played that year, with gusto, zest, daring and pace, was reflected on the streets of the capital city as the hours to the kick-off against Ireland ticked down. It was different in 2008: the weather invited everyone indoors, Wales were more functional than they had been three years before and it was not only the grey-haired and balding who knew what it was like to celebrate a Grand Slam. Welsh rugby followers had perhaps became blasé about success in the 1970s, with Grand Slams, Triple Crowns and championship titles seeming to occur with the frequency of Christmas, but given what had happened in 2006 and 2007, that was not a factor this time. A worker emerged from a hotel at the back of Greyfriars Road sporting a replica England shirt; no one bothered jeering. England might have been in the process of beating Ireland to finish second in the Six Nations, but they had never been in the hunt for the title. Like the red-rosed shirt being worn in Cardiff, their glory had faded. For Wales, it had become about more than merely beating England.

'As each victory this season has edged us closer to the prize, so the clichés have poured out on the alleged hysteria of the supporting populace, as if we are all slightly simple,' wrote Carolyn Hitt in the *Western Mail* on the morning of the France match:

> You can see why they might jump to this conclusion. After all, there was a bloke at the Italy game wearing head-to-toe pink spandex. And, granted, the build-up to 2005 was pretty full on. How could it not be? If you wait 27 years for something, you are bound to go doolally when it's finally in reach. Yet 2008 is different. Special . . . exciting . . . but still different. We're not bonkers this time. Welsh rugby can be a mad, mad world but a certain serenity has surrounded the countdown to the big day. It's still a lovely feeling. Not the raw emotion of three years ago, more a sense of how it should be . . . This season has brought something new. There has been a discernible shift in the supporters' mindset. A calmer optimism, somehow.

The *Western Mail* reported that a pair tickets for the France match were being sold on an Internet auction site for £1,000, nearly ten times their face value; after the match, the same site had ticket stubs attracting bidders. Fans without tickets could watch the game live on a big screen that was put up outside Cardiff City Hall, but little more than 300 people turned up because of the pouring rain, well short of the 7,000 capacity; the offer of free red waterproof ponchos for the first 500 supporters who bought a drink from the bar was not enough to beat the weather. That was good news for the city's traders, because an estimated £10 million was spent in the city centre that day. Cardiff International Airport saw 6,000 passengers above the average pass through the arrivals gate, and the match attracted an average television audience of 875,000 viewers in Wales, compared to 725,000 in 2005, the highest figure for a rugby match since records had started 15 years before. Nearly one million viewers tuned in for the final 15 minutes of the match, virtually one-third of Wales's population. A two-night stay for two in a city-centre flat was being offered for £600, with a fridge full of lager included in the price. Inside the ground, part of the pre-match entertainment comprised a contest between five Welsh choirs to determine which one would lead the singing for the Welsh national anthem. The choirs were made up of supporters of Wales's four professional regional sides with the fifth representing north Wales and captained by the Wales forwards coach Robin McBryde. The north won.

Sitting in the VIP box was François Fillon, the prime minister of France, and his wife Penelope. They were cheering for different sides: Mme Fillon was born in Llanover, near Abergavenny, and she got married in 1980 at her local parish church. 'I will be trying hard not to get too excited, but I have been following Wales, and it is nice to see them doing well,' she said. 'I think people in France understand there is always a part of you that you cannot give up. Whenever there is a country from the British Isles playing, my heart tends towards them, so I was secretly supporting England against France last month.'

It was an afternoon when both the Fillons could end up celebrating victory: France had a chance of claiming the title, but they needed to win by a margin of at least 20 points because of Wales's superior points difference. The chances were that Wales would win the title, even in defeat, although Shane Williams would have been mindful of his first cap, against France back in 2000, Wales's first match not only in the Six Nations, but in the championship at the Millennium Stadium. He came on as a replacement, quickly made a mistake that led to a try and was part of a team that lost 36–3. 'He came on that day and none of us knew who he was,' said the former France outside-half Thomas Castaignède. 'Afterwards, at the reception, he'd had a few beers and was a bit wobbly, so I said to someone that I'd be surprised if he had much of a future ahead of him.' In 2008, Wales had still to defeat France in the Six Nations in Cardiff, their previous success coming at the old National Stadium 12 years before when they had gone into the game looking to avoid a successive whitewash rather than a Grand Slam. Times had changed.

Gatland had announced two changes from the side that had defeated Ireland, maintaining his record of always shaking things up after a victory. Huw Bennett, who had pulled out on the morning of the match in Dublin because of illness, returned at hooker in place of Matthew Rees, but the headlines were generated by the decision to restore James Hook at outside-half, with Stephen Jones returning to the bench. Both players had started two matches, and it was an indication that Gatland intended Wales to keep the ball in hand. He had insisted that the roof be shut, with the weather forecast promising heavy rain at the end of the week and into Saturday, and when the request was put to France on the Wednesday, they agreed with alacrity.

For the first time since he had arrived in Wales, emotion seemed to settle on Gatland's face as he admitted that the call at outside-half had been one of the toughest he had had to make in his coaching career. 'Stephen is gutted, and I really feel for him,' said Gatland. 'It was an agonising decision to make, but we felt that James would offer more of a threat in attack. I do not get any pleasure out of telling a player he has been dropped. It was a tough call, but Stephen took it on the chin. I have a huge amount of respect for him as a player and as an individual, and leaving him out was one of the hardest things I have done as a coach. It is a downside of the job, and it does not make you happy when you let players down, but you have to make these calls sometimes.'

Gatland said that he would have considered dropping the scrum-half Mike Phillips had Wales lost at Croke Park following the player's yellow card for an act of foul play just before half-time. 'I spoke to Mike after the game,' he went on. 'We have tried to improve the side in a number of areas and discipline is one of them. I have told him not to get involved in anything like that again, and he has to learn from it. If the result had been different, he could have lost his place.' Phillips had been outstanding in defeat against France in Cardiff in 2006, taking a rare opportunity to start when Dwayne Peel was injured, by making a number of telling breaks. It turned out to be Scott Johnson's final match in charge as caretaker head coach before he returned to Australia, and for the first time that Six Nations his side had played with pragmatism. As defenders stepped wide, expecting Wales to move the ball swiftly away from the breakdown, as had become their trademark, Phillips shot through gaps and instilled doubt where there had been certainty. 'I told Mike a few weeks ago that he could become the most imposing scrum-half in world rugby. He told me he already was! He also said he was the best looking. He does not lack confidence, but what we have looked to add to his game is balance, taking on defences at the right time.' Gatland admitted that good fortune with injuries had been a factor in Wales's rise, but a week after the victory over France, Phillips damaged knee ligaments playing for the Ospreys in the EDF Energy Cup semi-final against Saracens at the Millennium Stadium and needed an operation that would sideline him for six months.

Gatland could no longer deflect talk about the Grand Slam, but he also widened the debate. 'We have won the Triple Crown, but it would be hollow to claim the title without beating France,' he said. 'We have a historic opportunity, which we intend to grab with both hands. The events of 2005 might give us an advantage, because the players know what the build-up to a big game like this is like, but it is not about the past. We have to move forward, and we have to appreciate that we still have to test ourselves against the big southern-hemisphere teams. We can only measure ourselves against the best sides. We have two Tests in South Africa in June, and we will face South Africa, New Zealand and Australia in Cardiff next November. We will find out then whether we are closing the gap. We have to maintain what we have managed to achieve in this championship and that is improve with every game.'

The media conference was being held in a small room at the Vale of Glamorgan Hotel. It would have been spacious enough twelve months before when Wales had lost, rather than won, their opening four matches and the only interest to the media appeared to be whether Hook would get a go at outside-half and whether Gareth Jenkins would survive until the World Cup. But success had generated a news frenzy, and there was not enough space in which to conduct separate interviews for the morning, evening and Sunday newspapers as well as accommodate the broadcasters. The radio and television crews went outside, where the wind was blowing with a fury. As the doors to a patio area were opened, a rickety construction housing sponsors logos that had been placed behind where Gatland had been sitting, in full camera view, blew over, but a reporter broke its fall before it reached the centre Tom Shanklin, who was sitting at a nearby table answering questions.

A number of morning newspaper reporters had requested access to Gavin Henson. Approaches made days before had been met with equivocal replies, and as Shanklin sat praising his centre colleague, no one knew whether Henson would be made available. It was a decision for the management to make, so the whispers went, and they could not make up their minds. Henson had spoken only to Sunday newspaper reporters, once, in the build-up to a Six Nations match, while he had been brought down for the mornings after the victory over Italy. He was the obvious player to feature ahead of France. He had not started a Six Nations match between the end of the 2005 campaign and the start of the current campaign, and he had a remarkable record in the championship: he had been in the starting line-up on nine occasions and been on the winning side each time. He was looking for the perfect ten, even if he would be doing so from inside-centre.

Eventually, scurrying feet signalled Henson's arrival. He sat in the seat just vacated by Shanklin and was immediately surrounded by reporters jostling for position. He was flanked by two members of the Welsh Rugby Union's communications department, who acted as minders to intercept any dodgy questions, as if mindful of Oscar Wilde's remark: 'In the old days, men had the rack, now they have the press . . . The public have an insatiable demand to know everything. Except what is worth knowing. Journalism, conscious of this, and having tradesman-like habits, supplies their demands.'

You could not help but wonder whether, in the attempt to protect Henson from his own honesty, Wales were in danger of giving him a complex. But he appeared relaxed and, after a few gentle deliveries, was asked about Warren Gatland.

'It is a great hurdle to clear when a new coach comes in and says he thinks highly of you,' he said. 'You want to repay the faith. The coaching team have been refreshing, and I am savouring their new ideas and different techniques. I am learning at every training session, and I love the intensity which now surrounds us. I have never trained like this before. Very little talking goes on; it is all about concentration, and it has given us a mental toughness, which everyone could see in the last five minutes against Ireland last weekend when we closed the game out. I don't think we would have been able to do that before. It is just great to be involved again, unlike the last couple of years. I have been determined to take my chance and stay in the side. I feel I should have a lot more caps [he had twenty-seven], having made my debut seven years ago, but I am nowhere near the end of my career, and I want to get as many caps as I can. That means playing well.'

Gatland had earlier blamed the media for the problems that had overwhelmed Henson after the 2005 Grand Slam to the point that it had been uncertain whether the centre would ever represent his country again. 'The media have been 99 per cent of the problem with Gavin,' said the head coach, who felt that Henson had the potential to become the leading player in his position in the world. 'They have built him up and run stories about him and his partner, and it must be difficult for him at times to balance that side of it with being a rugby player. I have treated him as a normal member of the squad, giving him coaching and direction. He has responded fantastically.'

When told about Gatland's contention that he had it in him to become the number one number 12 in the world, Henson sat back and reflected. He had not been asked about his wilderness years, the storm his autobiography created or the pain of rejection before the 2007 World Cup. He measured his words. 'To show you are the best centre in the world, you have to go to the World Cup and prove yourself against the best players,' he said. 'I have not done that yet. When you play at international level, you want to be the best in the world in your position, but I have a long way to go.' It was a statement that confirmed something Shanklin had said a few minutes before: 'I think Gavin is maturing, and he seems to be so highly motivated. He has not been hitting the headlines too much, but the way he has been playing has been fantastic. He is getting on with the job, and one feature of his game is that he would rather put other people in for tries than score himself. Gavin's return has taken a bit of pressure off me, and I think we form a good partnership.'

France announced their team the day after Wales. Their head coach Marc Lièvremont, having opted to use the Six Nations to look at as many players as he could, plumped for experience in making six changes from the side that had defeated Italy, although the wing Aurélien Rougerie was left out of the 22 with the full-back Cédric Heymans relegated to the bench. Lièvremont, who had played at the Millennium Stadium for France in the 1999 World Cup final against Australia, admitted that his side's prospects of winning the Six Nations were slim. 'It is a lot to ask to win by 20 points, but denying Wales the Grand Slam would be nice,' he said. 'We have put together the best team we could to win. We will play as we have all tournament, looking to retain the ball and dictate the pace of the game. We always want to take the initiative, even if we have not always managed it perfectly. Letting Wales run at us in a stadium where the atmosphere will be white-hot will be a sure way to defeat. It will be a true challenge to play in what is sure to be a hostile environment.'

The France scrum-half Jean-Baptiste Élissalde preferred to look at Wales as a team that had failed to qualify for the World Cup quarter-finals rather than one that was sitting at the top of the Six Nations. 'This is not the All Blacks or Australia we are talking about here,' he said. 'We haven't lost in Cardiff for ages. And when we played them in Cardiff before the World Cup last year, we put 30 points on them. Their players have not changed, just the staff. Their focus is more channelled, but looking at the level of their rugby and ours, there is not normally a comparison. We must not let ourselves be submerged by the wave of red that is going to crash into us at the start of the match, especially as there is no need to be worried. We must not go there feeling we are going to be the victims, rather the favourites. We saw in the World Cup in France that you can freeze in your own backyard when so much emotion is swirling around. I hope it will be the same with the Welsh. They are playing for the Grand Slam in front of their own public – that does not happen to them very often.'

Shaun Edwards revealed in his column in *The Guardian* that the debate in the Wales camp had been whether, after four successive victories, they should change what had been a successful game plan to cope with the very different threat posed by France:

The question was put to the players this week, because, depending on their choice, it could mean another week of pain. My abiding memory of the Six Nations so far is not the opening-day win against England when we came off the ropes, but it's of our second row Ian Gough after the record victory over Italy in the third round. He was ashen. He had lost 11 lb, and he was hurting. In the changing-room, others were celebrating, dancing around, but Ian was slumped and spent. He had given everything, was grey and needed attention from the medics. But he'd done everything asked of him. So far in the championship, we've kept the ball in play, kicking deep instead of for touch. In some rugby union matches, there might be between 30 and 32 minutes of actual play. Against Ireland, those tactics kept the ball in play for 42 minutes, and that demands a certain level of fitness and commitment. It's no coincidence that we came strong in the second half against England, Italy and then at Croke Park. But France are different. The last time they played at the Millennium Stadium they knocked New Zealand, the favourites, out of the World Cup, and now they come to Wales with attack in mind, needing to win by 20 points to retain their title. So do you kick to them?

Edwards was aware of the threat posed by two of France's back three, Anthony Floch and Julien Malzieu, after his Wasps side had lost in Clermont Auvergne in the Heineken Cup earlier in the season and then had to withstand a second-half fightback by the French side in the return game at Adams Park. He continued:

This week Warren Gatland asked the players whether they wanted another week of the pain game. I'm not going to say what they answered, but the mere asking of the question illustrated the give and take in the squad. Warren is the boss and has the final say, but he doesn't make the mistake of believing he has all the correct answers. On defensive matters, I've disagreed a few times, and he's also a willing listener to Rob Howley, Neil Jenkins and, particularly when it comes to the lineout, Robin McBryde. So it's not all rule from the top. However, the players understand that the coaches are united and that any criticism is constructive and designed to make them better and fitter. They've bought into the ethos and have learned astonishingly quickly. It's almost scary how fast they picked up on what was wanted. But don't expect any complacency tomorrow, even if the game plan is the one voted for by the players. Collectively we were too slow out of the blocks against England, Italy and Ireland. That can't happen again, because you can't go behind to France.

It was Wales's 100th international at the Millennium Stadium, 100 years after they had won their first Grand Slam, while the Triple Crown had been achieved on Gatland's 99th day in charge. Wales had started tentatively in their Grand Slam match against Ireland in 2005, calming down after the prop Gethin Jenkins had charged down Ronan O'Gara's clearance kick to score their opening try. 'If I was compiling a DVD of my favourite rugby moments so far, that try would be at the top of the list,' said Jenkins, who was about to win his 58th cap and draw level with Garin Jenkins as Wales's most capped front rower. 'I don't score very often. The occasion was incredible, and the day just flew by. Everyone talks about Grand Slam fever, but you have got to cut yourself off and laugh at how mad people are getting. We are playing a different style to three years ago: we off-loaded a lot then and looked for space. That still happens, but we have more of a power game now. No one expected it to work so quickly, especially after the World Cup, but winning breeds confidence, and we have not looked back since beating England.'

Jenkins was one of seven players facing France who had started against Ireland in 2005: Shanklin, Henson, Adam Jones, Ryan Jones and the Williamses, Shane and Martyn, were the others. Shane Williams was looking for the try that would take him to 41 for Wales and break Gareth Thomas's record, but he had never scored against France. The only match he had not scored in in 2008 was against England, unlike three years before when he had scored the only try of the opening game in that year's championship. Williams had turned thirty-one three days after scoring two tries against Italy in the third round, but he looked sharper than ever. 'I said after the Italy game that Shane was a one in ten million player,' said Shaun Edwards the week after the Grand Slam had been secured. 'I was wrong. I should have said one in fifty million, one hundred million even. He has dazzled for us and scored some remarkable tries, but what has impressed me most about him is that he does not make mistakes. He does not give the ball away or throw out wild passes when collared by a defender. He is a role model for other wings, because he never hangs around waiting for the ball. He goes looking for it and pops up all over the place. I have never seen anyone like him in either code of rugby. He is belting, as we like to say in Wigan.'

And it was to be Williams who made the difference on a tension-filled afternoon. 'Shane proves that rugby is not just a game for the big man, and he has again disproved all the prejudices that have grown up over the years about the need for size,' said the former Wales and Lions wing Gerald Davies on the eve of the France game. 'It is also a game for the man with great talent, the man with quick feet and a quick mind. What I like about him is that he assesses the moment to perfection. He must be the man of the tournament.' He was confirmed as such four days after the end of the championship, and it had been another Williams, Martyn, who had been the player of the tournament in 2005. The flanker was to finish the scoring against France with the first try scored by a Wales forward in that year's competition, a far cry from three years before when seven of Wales's sixteen tries had been claimed by members of the pack. It showed how Wales's game had evolved from one that was loose and often unstructured to one that had forwards hitting rucks and mauls and doing a lot more grunt work. They might have been seen with the ball in their hands a lot less, but they were doing more running and took considerably more contact.

In the build-up to the final two rounds, Edwards had brought in Paul Stridgeon, the former Commonwealth Games wrestler who was a strength and conditioning coach with Warrington and who had worked with Edwards at Wasps, to take a gym session. 'A lot of the boys said it was like an out-of-body experience because it was so hard,' said Shanklin. 'We had to do a circuit in the gym and then one in the Barn, in groups of four, and it took twenty-five minutes non-stop. It took you 20 minutes to recover. They want us to be that tired. The theory is that if we are not as tired in a game as we were that day, then we still have more to give.

The mentality the coaches are trying to drill into us is to work through the pain. They are getting us to toughen up. I twisted my ankle against Ireland but didn't want to go down until the clock stopped.'

Wales's conditioning was again to have a telling impact in the final quarter after a cat-and-mouse opening against France. Les Bleus made the stronger start but, after finding no way through a defence marshalled by Henson, who was tackling by example, resorted to kicking, and their outside-half David Skrela, who arrived with a reputation for reliability, slowly unravelled – one of his restarts actually went backwards. Skrela's father, Jean-Claude, had played in the 1978 match in Cardiff at wing forward when Wales won their third Grand Slam in seven years.

Wales made their first real thrust after eight minutes when they moved to the right on halfway, and Hook deceived the defence with a pass out of the back of his hand, earning himself a nudge from the second row Jérôme Thion. The ball found its way to the wing Mark Jones, who sprinted into the France 25. Lee Byrne was supporting him on the inside and would have had a free run to the line with a timed pass, but Jones cut inside and slipped on the greasy surface. Wales had the consolation of a penalty, and Hook accepted the three points. France continued to enjoy a supply of possession but, surprisingly, they did not use runners from deep and kept moving the ball on or two out with a flat line, and the Wales defenders were not troubled by doubt. Hook hooked a second penalty attempt before converting a third. Wales were 6–0 up with 18 minutes gone, but a mistake from the restart forced Martyn Williams to hold on to the ball, and Élissalde made it 6–3. Hook restarted long, the France flanker Thierry Dusautoir made a hash of trying to pick the ball up near his own line and a pile-up developed that ended with a Wales penalty when the number 8 Julien Bonnaire rashly charged in from the side in front of the referee Marius Jonker. Hook stepped up: 9–3.

France started to enjoy their best period of the match but found themselves invited up blind alleys. The statistics after the match showed that France had the ball for 33 minutes compared with Wales's 22 but spent most of the game in their own half, with Wales's kicking out of hand again proving effective. France completed one hundred and fifty-one passes compared to Wales's eighty-one, but made just one line break as opposed to Wales's four. France won the ball one hundred and ten times in open play, but only six times in Wales's twenty-five. Wales won the ball 74 times in open play and did so in France's 25 on 14 occasions. If France had the ball, while Wales had the territory, it was Wales who played in the right areas.

Wales had lost a player to the sin-bin just before the interval in Dublin, and they saw yellow again in first-half stoppage time when James Hook tackled the flanker Fulgence Ouedraogo on Wales's 25. The forward was starting his descent when Henson arrived and made a high tackle, accepting his punishment with a fatalistic shrug. Élissalde made it 9–6 with the last kick of the half, and France would have a one-man advantage for the first ten minutes of the second period. The scores were level when Henson returned, Élissalde kicking a third penalty after Hook had missed from 30 yards, wide on the left. The game was stop-start and the question, as it went into the last quarter, with Stephen Jones replacing Hook, was whether Wales had been overcome by nerves or whether they were biding their time.

It proved to be the latter and Wales, who had been so

reluctant to introduce the blitz defence under their previous two coaches, made Edwards's system pay. France had a scrum just inside their own half and tried to work a move through Bonnaire. As Henson and Shanklin rushed up, Skrela's pass went behind the centre Yannick Jauzion, who, if he had caught the ball, would have had an inviting gap in front of him. Shane Williams kicked the loose ball into France's 25 and set off in pursuit. Under pressure from Floch, he hacked the ball towards the France line. Élissalde tried to ankle tap the wing, which would have earned a yellow card and a penalty try if he had been successful, but he could only watch the ball bounce off the post and over the line before Williams pounced on it for his record 41st try for Wales. He had said in Dublin that it was time he scored a try under the posts, and Jones's conversion made it 16–9. As had happened so often under Gatland, a combination of pressure when not in possession and the predatory instinct of Williams had yielded a score. The crowd relaxed, and the singing started when a Jones penalty made it 19–9.

France, however, were not quite done. There had been a number of crucial moments in the campaign – Bennett getting an arm under the ball as Paul Sackey tried to ground it at Twickenham, Gonzalo Canale's knock-on for Italy, Phillips's try-saving tackle on Shane Horgan at Croke Park and Martyn Williams's professional foul on Eoin Reddan – but if one moment summed up the difference between Wales in 2005 and Gatland's model, it came ten minutes from the end against France when handling errors gave the French a scrum ten yards from the Wales line for their best attacking position of the evening. As the France back row anticipated their move, Wales scrummaged as an eight and drove their opponents back to claim the ball and relieve the pressure. 'I think it was the turning point of the game,' said the prop Adam Jones, who before the Ireland match had swapped his shaggy hairstyle for a braided, corn-row look. 'Not many teams do that to a French scrum, and it was one of my best moments in rugby. It showed how in two months we had gained a harder edge.'

Although the replacement scrum-half Dimitri Yachvili was soon to kick a penalty to make it 19–12, the indignity of being shoved off their own ball marked the end for France. Jones landed a forty-five-yard penalty two minutes before the start of stoppage time, and the Grand Slam was secure. There was still time for Mark Jones, who was looking for his first try of the tournament, to receive a pass from Alun Wyn Jones after a lineout near the Wales line and swerve in and out of tackles to go on a 90-yard run before he was hauled down just short of the line. Wales were not to be denied, and Martyn Williams, who had put in some relieving kicks from outside-half, popped up at scrum-half and darted through a gap from 25 yards out to confirm Wales's superiority and seal a Man of the Match performance little more than two months after he had come out of international retirement. Jones's conversion made it 29–12, Wales's biggest victory over France in Cardiff since 1950 in what was another Grand Slam match. Cue the fireworks.

After Ryan Jones had been presented with the Six Nations trophy, he invited Gatland and the other coaches to join the players on the podium in celebration. Gatland shook his head. He had from the start drawn a line between the players and the management. He laid down what he expected from his squad, but the players were the only ones who could deliver. As Shaun Edwards said when an interviewer praised him for the meanest defence in the championship, 'I never made a tackle.' The players had been through the most physically and mentally gruelling two months of their careers. Gatland was telling them it was their success and to enjoy it while he and his fellow coaches looked on, as they had done when Stridgeon was testing the players' endurance to the limit.

After the presentation, Ryan Jones gathered his players together. 'I said to them that my proudest moment was not lifting the trophy on behalf of them but of being in the changing-room with them, because I know how hard they worked to get us to that podium,' he said. 'The turning point for me today was when we pushed France off their own scrum ball. It was the moment we knew they had cracked, that we were better than they were and that it was our game. There were huge pats on the back for the tight five and rightful recognition of the effort they had put in in all five matches.'

In the *Daily Telegraph* the following Monday, Brendan Gallagher wrote:

> Who knows where it will all end – but I definitely have a theory where it all started. Stradey Park, 11 a.m. on 15 November last year, a glorious day borrowed from late summer when 10,000 Wales diehards gathered at Ray Gravell's funeral and the rest of the rugby nation crowded around their office TVs for an hour. Beforehand, many thought such a tribute over the top and a tad embarrassing, but, in fact, with the memory of Gravell as a catalyst, it turned into the most glorious joyful reaffirmation of Wales's love affair with rugby, a huge and tangible lift following the World Cup. The movers and shakers of Welsh rugby – players and administrators – left feeling good about themselves again. Shoulders squared, they would go back to work and sort the bloody mess out. And since then it has all been good.

10

NEVER BE LIKE YESTERDAY

I have travelled the paths of desire,
Following smoke and remembering fire.
The night is falling, the path is receding.
I don't need to see where it's leading.

Julie Flanders

16 MARCH 2008. SOME WALES PLAYERS ARE emerging from the Vale of Glamorgan Hotel. It is 10.30 a.m., the morning after the night before. It marks a contrast with the end of the previous tournament they had taken part in when the management and players were preparing to leave Pornichet and the World Cup, the mourning after the plight before. Martyn Williams is preparing to leave for home: before he gets into his car, he reflects that he is standing in a place he has been before, three years previously when the air was creamy with the scent of success and the promise of more to come.

Wales had won the Grand Slam, playing with a freedom and a flourish some feared had become obsolete in international rugby. They had emerged from a deep depression that had started when Warren Gatland's Waikato had beaten them in the summer of 1988 and that had only intermittently let in some light since. The Triple Crown of 1988 and the 1994 Five Nations title proved to be one-offs rather than springboards, and so it was to be after 2005. The coaches that tournament, Mike Ruddock, Scott Johnson, Clive Griffiths and Andrew Hore, would all have gone before the start of the 2006–07 season. Dreams turned into ashes, ashen faces and ashamedness. When it came to beating themselves up, Wales still had few rivals on the world stage.

'I said in the team meeting after we had beaten France that we did not handle success well three years ago,' said Williams. 'We didn't move forward, but I don't think we'll be allowed to let up this time, and I hope this will just be the starting point. A number of the boys are in their prime and have several years left ahead of them.' Much had been made in 2005 about the Welsh way of playing: it was too loosely defined as throwing the ball around and being expansive, a theory that failed to take into account the way Wales and Welsh clubs had played through the years, with an instinctive feel for the game that allowed them to win any which way. And the Welsh way was about winning: in 2005, that meant compensating for Wales's relative lack of bulk and power up front by avoiding contact as often as possible; in 2008, it meant being attritional, having powers of endurance and waiting for the final 20 minutes when opponents would tire and Welsh predators would pounce.

In the five matches combined, Wales scored sixty-seven points in the final quarter and conceded six: 17–0 against England, 13–0 against Scotland, 14–0 against Italy, 3–3 against Ireland and 20–3 against France. The Grand Slam was won as much in the gym as on the training field. 'To come out of the tournament having conceded just two tries is so un-Welsh,' said Williams. Yes and no.

Just before Wales won the 2005 Grand Slam, the former England and Lions coach Dick Best did not earn himself the freedom of any of the Welsh cities when he said that the success had been built on a foundation of sand and that it would only prove temporary before sinking from view. He was concerned that the Lions would be tempted to take a glut of Welsh players with them to New Zealand that summer and wreck their chances of doing well because, to him, the series would hinge on the forward exchanges, and the land of the long white cloud would be no place for showing off. Wales beat Ireland a couple of days after Best made his remarks, and letters columns in newspapers were full of acidic advice for the man who in his coaching days had been known as 'Sulphuric'. Most of the Grand Slam team did go with the Lions – Gareth Thomas captained the side in the last two Tests after Brian O'Driscoll returned home injured – and the All Blacks won the series 3–0.

Best was more sanguine about Wales's prospects after the 2008 success. 'I think it is there for everyone to see that there is a lot more substance to Wales this time,' he said. 'They looked anything but champions in the first half against England but had a complete metamorphosis during the interval and never looked back. They generated a huge amount of confidence, but they should have been driven into the ground at Twickenham. They left the place a different team, and they became steadily more impressive as the tournament went on. I could not see Wales building on the 2005 Grand Slam, and even though I was pilloried from Chepstow to Cardigan for saying so, I feel I was proved right. But under their 2008 management team, I can see Wales moving on. I know Shaun Edwards better than Warren Gatland, and he has an insatiable appetite for winning. Edwards has brought a different dimension to Wales and has been good for them. He got on to the players' cases straight away, and there was no self-congratulation after beating England, as there would probably have been in times past. He instilled discipline into Wales and earned the respect of the players in return. The concern for Wales at the end of the championship would have been to tie down Edwards until the 2011 World Cup. England missed a trick by letting Edwards go; losing him was a national disgrace.'

England finished second in the Six Nations, their best finish for five years, but even though it followed on from their achievement in reaching the World Cup final, the Rugby Football Union decided that the national management team needed to be shaken up. There were concerns about leadership, selections, tactics and man-management. Brian Ashton was regarded as a second in command rather than a leader, and, after a review of the championship campaign, Twickenham decided to appoint a team manager to oversee the set-up and give him carte blanche to appoint the coaching team. The 2003 World Cup-winning captain Martin Johnson was sounded out and agreed to talks. It put Ashton's future in doubt and raised the possibility that England would look to persuade Edwards to come into the fold. Edwards was interviewed on television after the victory over France and, asked about his future, gave a cryptic response that hinted that he would not reject an approach from England out of hand. The Welsh Rugby Union had opened talks with him over a contract that would run until the end of the 2011 World Cup, but Edwards wanted a new deal with Wasps to run in parallel. Part of the salary Edwards received from Wales was kept by Wasps, as compensation for releasing him on a part-time basis, and he felt the two contracts would have to be interlinked. An approach from England would provoke extreme soul-searching: he felt a loyalty, as well as a friendship, to Gatland and appreciated that Wales had allowed him to fulfil his ambition of coaching at international level, but he had always hoped to become involved with England at some point. One source of comfort for the WRU was that Edwards would have to leave Wasps if he accepted a position with England, under a rule drawn up by Premier Rugby, and the key behind his coming to Wales was that the job was part time.

'With Edwards on board, Wales have a strong, united management team,' said Best. 'Five of their next six fixtures after the 2008 Six Nations, three against South Africa, including two on tour, New Zealand and Australia, would ordinarily have been too much for them, but the way they played in the championship, with a hard edge and refusing to take a backward step, suggested to me that they would have a big chance in the backyard of the world champions, who were always going to be in transition after their exploits in France. I think Wales have the makings of a very, very good side. They have long been regarded as fragile defensively, but Gatland's selection policy made sure there was intense competition for places and everyone who pulled on their Wales jersey gave everything they had. They are a team which plays for each other, and you can tell that they enjoy it.'

Ian McGeechan, Edwards's director of rugby at Wasps, also felt Wales were better prepared to cope with success than they had been at any time in the previous 20 years. 'I cannot see a repeat of what happened in 2005,' he said. 'I think this is a start for Wales, not an end. They will get stronger. They evolved with every game in the Six Nations and ended up being the best side in attack and defence. They showed a clarity of thought and that reflected on the way they had been trained and in the tactics they adopted. Warren and Shaun made an immediate impact, but the role of Robert Howley should not be understated. He would have provided the initial link between the two new coaches and the players, and it was always going to be a case of how quickly the management and the squad generated a chemistry. It turned out to be almost immediate, and I thought the selection for the first game at Twickenham was brilliant. Warren had not had much time with the players in the run-up to the start of the Six Nations, and by picking 13 Ospreys for England, he was not only fielding a group of players who knew each other well, but was ensuring that Shaun's blitz defence system had an optimum chance of succeeding, because the Ospreys were the only one of the Welsh regions to use it. Beating England away was a huge start, but I know that Shaun would have got stuck into the players on the Monday and homed in on their mistakes and stressed what they needed to put right.'

Wales's success in the Six Nations put Gatland in the frame to coach the Lions in South Africa in 2009. After the 2001 tour to Australia, when the then Wales coach Graham Henry had become the first person from outside the British Isles to coach the Lions, only to return home so exhausted that within seven months he would be back in New Zealand, the WRU passed a policy that prevented their coaching staff being hired by the Lions. Edwards, by virtue of his part-time role, was an exception, but there were concerns in the union, even though the manager in South Africa would be a WRU board member, Gerald Davies, that Wales would be better served by Gatland not going, or at the very least not being the head coach. Pundits suggested a Wasps trio of McGeechan (who had coached the Lions in 1989, 1993 and 1997 and had been a member of Clive Woodward's management team in 2005), Gatland and Edwards, with McGeechan heading up the coaching team. 'My priority is Wales,' said Gatland the day after Wales had won the Grand Slam. 'It would be a huge honour to be asked to do the job, but there would be a lot of things to think about, starting with the selection of the players. In 2005, Wales did not have enough, and in 2001 they probably had too many. There is a lot of politics involved, and it is all about balance.'

Gatland's first tour with Ireland was to South Africa in 1998. They lost their two tests in Bloemfontein and Pretoria, the venues he was to revisit with Wales ten years later. 'We have won the Grand Slam, but we do not want to stop there,' he said. 'You have to test yourself against the best teams in the world, and South Africa are number one at the moment. I honestly believe that this Wales team over the next twelve months to two years will become a very good side that will be difficult to beat and won't be afraid to play anyone. We've made a lot of progress in the last seven weeks. The players have given more than we, as coaches, have asked of them. They've improved from game to game, but we are still going to have to do a lot of hard work. I am very aware of what happened after 2005, and it is essential that we build on our success in the Six Nations. My work starts now, and no one will be resting on their laurels. If we sit back, we will get caught. It is tough enough winning in South Africa but even harder to do so at altitude, but we are not going there in trepidation, and I am going to take the strongest squad I can. We have to keep our feet on the ground and test ourselves against the southern-hemisphere teams. We have to play the best in the world to learn the intensity. I agree with people who say that it's been a weak Six Nations, with teams in transition and turmoil – that often happens after a World Cup. Wales have achieved a lot of milestones, including our biggest Six Nations win in the victory over Italy and a record victory against France. There's a lot to build on. If you look at England's World Cup success in 2003, it was based on regular tours of the southern hemisphere with a mindset to go out and challenge those teams. The great thing is that the WRU are going out and trying to arrange fixtures against these sides that will build the platform for us ahead of the 2011 World Cup.'

Gatland had mapped out his programme for the Six Nations campaign some weeks before the start of the tournament, and he catered for the smallest detail. In 2006, after Wales had opened the defence of their Six Nations title against England at Twickenham and been well beaten after collapsing in the final quarter, the squad stayed in London that night and had a row with the management over whether they should join some of the England players for an evening out. That was never going to be an issue in 2008, because Wales returned to the Vale of Glamorgan Hotel a few hours after the end of the victory at Twickenham, with Gatland wanting the players to have two full days of recovery. While the England players were being flogged for between two and three hours in training sessions, few of Gatland's workouts lasted an hour. Team meetings were also kept short. Every minute of work time was made to count. There was never any slacking. It had been the way he had operated at Wasps: the longer a season went on, the more he gave players time off to ensure they were at the peak during the final crucial month of a campaign when trophies were won and lost. In the week of the France match, training sessions lasted little more than 30 minutes.

In the *Sunday Telegraph*, Paul Ackford wrote:

> Some of Gatland's substitutions during the tournament were responses to the way the game was unfolding, some were pre-planned. Gatland had access to real-time information from three analysts who were studying six laptops. The coach went into a game prepared to replace one player from each row of the scrum because of the extra running required. Against France, Gethin Jenkins hit 48 rucks. In an earlier match, he managed less than half that number. That level of improvement was important and reflected the man-management skills that Gatland has displayed. The squad wanted to perform for him. Much has, quite rightly, been made of the contribution of Gatland and Edwards. In a radio interview, Ryan Jones referred to the pair as 'bad cop and badder cop'. Edwards has been likened by some players to Road Runner, the cartoon character who is never still. In meetings and on the practice pitches, Edwards is in your face, loud, brash, while Gatland is more discreet. Gatland's trick is sometimes to deliver his message from the back or

side of the team room. He talks softly, in contrast to Edwards, so that the players have to concentrate to take in what he has to say. They have been savvy. The reason James Hook was replaced by Stephen Jones after 56 minutes against France was because the coaches thought he was kicking too much, offering France respite. They wanted Wales to play flatter, to keep the ball on the pitch, to ask questions of France, and Jones came off the bench to execute those instructions.

Gatland preferred to play down his own contribution. 'We put a few structures in place and a bit of honesty and self-belief, but it was a team effort,' he said. 'It is all about the players; they are the ones who have a job to do for 80 minutes. A number of them have had it pretty tough in the last six to twelve months. The disappointment in the World Cup probably came about through missing a couple of shots at goal that cost them a quarter-final.' That Sunday evening, he was a guest on *Scrum V* and arrived, clutching the Six Nations Trophy, in a room populated by supporters from three rugby clubs. It was an informal setting, and he was one of four guests, the others being the former Wales captains Jonathan Davies and Gwyn Jones and the Ospreys New Zealand scrum-half Justin Marshall. It was hard to imagine Steve Hansen accepting such an invitation, but Gatland was at ease.

'If you had asked me 12 months ago if I would be sitting here, I would have said "You've got to be kidding me,"' said Gatland in a documentary on the Grand Slam screened by BBC Wales four days after the game against France. 'When I was trying to get Shaun on board, he was very cagey in terms of putting his name forward. "Wales? Look what happened to them in the World Cup and the Six Nations in the last couple of years," he said. "Do I want to get involved with that team?" We have always got on well. We are thinking about writing a book: the non-PC way of coaching by Gatland and Edwards. It has been a little more intense in Wales than I had anticipated. New Zealand is a goldfish bowl, but here people come up to you in the supermarket. You are aware that when the players take the field, there is a huge amount of responsibility on all of us.'

An essential difference between 2005 and 2008 was the significant improvement at regional level. Wales had won the first Grand Slam even though the regions were making a negligible impact in the Heineken Cup. Under Steve Hansen, Wales had virtually become a club side, locked together for long periods of time, and success had not come from the bottom up. In 2008, the Ospreys had made the quarter-finals of the Heineken Cup, along with Cardiff Blues, and the semi-finals of the EDF Energy Cup, progressing to the final a week after the Grand Slam had been won by defeating Saracens at the Millennium Stadium, while in 2007 Llanelli Scarlets had reached the semi-finals of the Heineken Cup, becoming in the process the first of the regions to advance from the pool stage. The Ospreys defeated Gloucester, who were then leading the Guinness Premiership, on their way to the last eight, and they won away to Ulster and Bourgoin, while the Blues doubled Bristol, drew at Harlequins and defeated Stade Français at home as they too made the knockout stage of Europe's premier club tournament for the first time. The way the Blues outmuscled a Bristol pack known for its physicality at the Memorial Stadium a couple of weeks before the start of the Six Nations offered a portent for the months ahead. 'When Wales do badly, the regions get a large slice of the blame, so when they do well maybe we should get a little credit,' said the Blues' head coach David Young. 'I am not suggesting for a moment that we get a lot of it, but some recognition would be nice. I've said before that I think we are too down on ourselves a lot of the time in Wales. We are not as bad as we sometimes think.'

The Ospreys had assembled a squad as strong as any in Europe, and in March 2008, Andrew Hore, Wales's conditioning coach for more than three years from June 2002, started work as the region's elite performance director, having spent a couple of years as the New Zealand Rugby Union's player development manager. He had been interviewed by the WRU the previous October for the governing body's new position of elite performance director, but there was disagreement over the job description. 'The Ospreys have really bought into the regional concept,' he said. 'They have come a long way in five years. There are ambitious, go-ahead people here involved at all levels who want to improve themselves and the region year on year. This is not a short-term job for me. I will be looking at all levels of the business from a rugby perspective with the aim of creating a strategic plan to move the Ospreys forward. I want to put in place world-leading practices. We want long-term success on and off the field, and it's my role to create a long-lasting legacy that will see the Ospreys established as a real world power.'

There was more concern about what was going on below the regions. 'There are still deep-rooted problems in Welsh rugby that need addressing,' wrote Phil Bennett in the *South Wales Evening Post*:

For instance, I went to see Felinfoel host Nantymoel last weekend and was sad to see the visitors were struggling for players. They are not alone. Across Wales, there are other examples of clubs finding it tough to run the same number of teams that they did not so long ago, with shortages of players in certain positions. Where is the next Shane Williams coming from? Shane came through at Amman United a decade ago, but have we got a system in place to make sure diamonds like him are spotted and polished up? The national coach also needs to look at our resources and pinpoint whether we are light in certain positions. He needs to be liaising with the regions, he needs to have a say on whether the structure is serving the national team adequately and he needs to be analysing the performances of Welsh players to make sure they are maintaining standards after the success of the Grand Slam. I hope Warren Gatland does not take charge of the Lions, because there is a lot of work for him to do in Wales. Someone needs to come out and say that the idea is a total non-starter.

The aftermath of 2005 ensured that there would be an emphasis on managing success. 'While we and our fans are justified in our celebrations, we can't let our Grand Slam or the public's euphoria detract from what we need to achieve next, and I can sum that up in one word: consistency,' said Tom Shanklin. 'Martyn Williams was right when he said we didn't handle the 2005 Grand Slam success well, and now I'd like us to follow up this repeat by driving ourselves on to nail down that consistency tag. The coaches have come in and been brilliant. They've drilled professionalism, attitude, work ethic and intensity into us, and that is what we have to keep doing. We have to keep pushing forward. We've had some great success, but we are the champions of the northern hemisphere and have to make sure from here on in we are more consistent. That has to be driven by the players and coaches, and I think we will do that. We've had this success and want more, and for that to happen we know we have to raise our standards again.'

The backs coach Rob Howley had been the captain of Wales when they won ten consecutive matches under Graham Henry in the New Zealander's first year in charge after arriving in August 1998. 'We must move on from our win, as we haven't played the world's top four teams yet,' said Howley. 'History shows that in Wales we like to enjoy the moment for too long, and that has been detrimental to the game. That won't happen again. Don't get me wrong, the players enjoyed a Grand Slam party on Saturday night and probably well into Sunday morning. And the coaches sunk plenty of champagne, but that has gone now. The Grand Slam has been achieved, and we have bigger targets. South Africa are the world champions, and they will be our acid test – they'll be the barometer to find out where we really are in world rugby. The Welsh coaching staff have a winning mentality; we want to be the best and that means beating the best. There's still a great deal of work to do before we can go to South Africa with a realistic opportunity of beating them. But the players have taken on board how hard we want to play and train, so they've an idea of the work that needs to be done if we're going to beat the world champions on their own turf. Warren has proved time and again that he is a master at putting the right coaching team and environment together. He knows trust and loyalty are the underlying indicators for success. We all challenge each other. Shaun challenges Warren, I challenge Shaun and Neil Jenkins challenges all of us – that's why it's working. Talent has never been a problem in Wales; it's just the direction.'

Wales failed to build on 2005 after a division among the management team led to the departure of Mike Ruddock. That was not an issue in 2008. 'There is unity among the coaching staff,' said Edwards. 'Players are the first to recognise if a management team is not together and pushing in the same direction. Warren is in charge, but he listens to me, Rob Howley, Neil Jenkins and Robin McBryde. The final decision is his. I wanted the roof open for France because I thought wet conditions would suit our blitz defence; Howlers is a worrier and felt that letting the rain in would diminish France's chances of winning by 20 points. Warren is a Kiwi optimist and said he wanted the roof shut so we could smash into the French and win the championship in style. We all backed him to the hilt. We brought in some systems we had applied at Wasps, and the players responded immediately. The big test of a squad is how players deal with being dropped, something the Lions have not always been able to react to. We had some disappointed players in the Six Nations, but they never let their personal feelings affect the team; any moaning they may have done was conducted in private. We all have a responsibility now to take this forward. We are going to the world champions South Africa, and we have a big responsibility as northern-hemisphere champions. We have no intention of being like a bunch of clowns. The Springboks are going to know they have been in a game.'

The *Western Mail* carried an editorial on the Monday

after the Grand Slam that started, 'This time we must get it right.' It asked whether the WRU had been right to sack Gareth Jenkins within hours of the defeat to Fiji and whether the union had been right to target and appoint a successor in double-quick time. It gave two resounding affirmatives to its own questions. The achievements of Gatland's Wales vindicated the WRU's swift action in going to New Zealand in pursuit of him, but one of the reasons that Wales had not followed up success on the infrequent occasions it had been sampled in the previous 20 years was the knee-jerk reaction to failure, with the 1988 dismissal of Tony Gray a graphic example of haste proving costly. The summary dismissal of Jenkins, whose contribution to Welsh rugby over nearly forty years as a player and coach at the sharp end was considerably greater than the vast majority of those who had sat in judgement on him, was unacceptable on two counts, never mind what was to happen in the new year. First, he should never have been subjected to the humiliation of being publicly sacked before the squad had left for Wales, forced to leave the team coach on his own before it arrived at the hotel to avoid the media scrum that was awaiting him. Second, it made it look as if he were solely responsible for the failure rather than taking into account the mess he had inherited, something that was of the WRU's, not his, making. The proper course of action would have been for the union's board of directors to meet early the following week and discuss not only Jenkins's future, but also how they could take measures to ensure that the position of head coach was never undermined from within again. Instead, the governing body chose to beat the Monday newspaper headline writers and strip Jenkins of his dignity as well as his job, an action that did not merit applause.

The WRU had ignored the warning signs in the last six months of Mike Ruddock's tenure as head coach, eventually finding itself unable to control events. In fairness to Roger Lewis, the union's chief executive, he was not around then, nor did he play any role in the appointment in 2006 of Jenkins, which was as muddled as the recruitment of Ruddock had been. The WRU empowered a five-man panel to find Ruddock's successor, but the board of directors, still unsettled by the events of a few months before, insisted on being presented with two names, rather than one as had previously been agreed. Jenkins had been dubbed the people's choice by the *Western Mail* and was duly given the job on a two-year contract. It was hardly surprising that the union indulged in some populism after the public-relations fiasco that followed Ruddock's departure, but it was an abdication of responsibility to allow Jenkins to carry the blame on his own when he failed to turn things around. It was more the humiliation of his employers than his, a sadly inevitable consequence of administrative mistakes. Jenkins would not have survived a review, and the WRU's search party would not have had to delay their flight to Auckland.

As Thomas Castaignède mused after the end of the Six Nations, 'Sporting success is a tightrope: it doesn't take a lot to fall off, and it doesn't need huge change to get back on.' Wales had attacked with aplomb in the World Cup but defended with despair, free-thinking anarchists. 'The players are pretty much the same, but suddenly they look more confident, precise and disciplined,' said Castaignède. 'That has to be mainly thanks to the reorganisation among the coaching staff, but the try that was not allowed for Paul Sackey against Wales at Twickenham changed the course of the tournament, the state of mind of both teams, the futures of the coaches and players. For me, it wasn't a try, but whatever you think it is surprising how half a centimetre one way or the other – or one man's judgement – can change so many destinies.'

Castaignède lamented the standard of the Six Nations and wondered if any one of the six teams was in a position to challenge the major southern-hemisphere unions, but it had been only a few months earlier that England had defeated Australia in the World Cup quarter-finals a couple of hours before France dumped out New Zealand in Cardiff. South Africa won the World Cup, but the only country among the traditional top eight they faced was England – twice. The 2007 World Cup was more interesting than any other not because of the overall quality of play, but because a number of unfancied countries, such as Tonga, Fiji and Georgia, rose above their also-ran billing. Fiji were level against South Africa in the quarter-final Wales missed out on and blew two try-scoring opportunities that would have put them ahead before succumbing to a late surge by the Springboks, who had in the group stage been given a fright by Tonga, while Georgia were hammering away at the Ireland line in the dying minutes, searching for the try that would have given them victory. There has long been a tendency in Europe to put the major southern-hemisphere teams on a pedestal, but Wales showed in the 2008 Six Nations that there was no discernible gap between them and Australia, while South Africa had opted to replace their head coach Jake White, even though he brought the Webb Ellis Trophy home with him, and named Peter de Villiers as his successor without having first agreed the terms of his contract. When it comes to rugby politics, Wales and South Africa are in a league of their own, despite England desperately playing catch-up.

There will be sterner Six Nations ahead for Gatland. France will at some point stop experimenting, and England will start to exploit the deep reservoir of talent that the Premiership, underpinned by the academies, has become. England won the 2008 Under-20s Six Nations and claimed a Grand Slam, playing rugby of such daring, skill and understanding that they seemed out of place in white jerseys. If Wales did not reflect the state of their domestic game in the 2005 Six Nations, then neither did England in 2008. Ireland parted company with Eddie O'Sullivan after a relatively successful six years, but some of his policies had become discredited, including making his national squad players available for Magners League matches mainly on derby days. Few of their golden generation of players, most of whom were first blooded by Gatland, will be around for the 2011 World Cup. Scotland only had two professional sides after disbanding Border Reivers at the end of the 2006–07 season and suffered from a consequent lack of depth, while Italy showed they had come to terms with the demands of the Six Nations without hitting on a winning formula.

Wales had the best team in 2008, and they also had many of the leading performers: Martyn Williams, out of retirement and bossing breakdowns; Ryan Jones, an undemonstrative captain who did not have to urge his troops to follow him; Ian Gough, the heartbeat of the side; Mike Phillips, lacking nothing in self-confidence but far more aware of the needs of the team; James Hook, without peer as an attacking outside-half; Gavin Henson and Tom Shanklin, reunited in midfield and as potent a combination as they had been in 2005; and Lee Byrne, infallible under the high ball and liable to return it with interest.

Not to forget Shane Williams. He was voted the player

of the tournament. His tries against Ireland and France had swung tight matches, and it was he who had shaken his teammates out of their stupor at Twickenham by taking a penalty quickly in his own 25 and darting away. He proved that small could be beautiful, and as he prospered, England's decision to fast track Lesley 'the Volcano' Vainikolo, the 6 ft 2 in., 17 st. 5 lb Tongan wing, backfired. Williams scored tries from everywhere, while Vainikolo, on the rare occasions he came infield, made few dents. If the Volcano looked extinct, Williams was molten lava. As he celebrated his award, Williams reflected on the vagaries of sport: 'There was a time in 2002 when I considered retiring. I was not playing for Wales, and I was fed up. I was convinced I would not get another cap and had had a gutful. I felt hard done by because Steve Hansen was not picking me, but now I know it was because I wasn't fit enough and I wasn't good enough. I was a bit immature and had to buck up my ideas. You have to be stubborn and bloody-minded, and I have always known that I am not one of those players who will get picked even when not in particularly good form. I have to be playing well.'

While Williams was talking, Gatland was in the air, on his way home for a short holiday in New Zealand. He had taken a flight of a different kind when staying in Roger Lewis's home the previous October and pondering whether to accept Wales's offer. 'I chartered a helicopter and told Warren I would show him Wales,' said Lewis. 'So, we flew around the country. I took him up the Rhondda valleys, I took him west of Llanelli, I took him to Newport, I took him over Swansea, I took him to meet my mother in a little mining village in the south, and I said, "Look, we're not going to make a decision this weekend. Let's just talk and get to know each other."' Gatland was immediately struck by one feature: 'We would fly over a village and then the next one, but there was no gap in between them,' he said. 'They were joined up. There was a rugby ground, then a mile away there would be another one and a mile on there was another one. I then knew that I was coming into a cauldron.'

A cauldron that is either bubbling furiously or one that contains a cold, congealed residue. Graham Henry was dubbed the 'Great Redeemer' within a couple of months of arriving in Wales. Gatland became the 'Resurrection Man' after reviving what had been written off before the start of the tournament as a corpse. They don't do moderation in Wales and quickly forget, as readers of the *Waikato Times* were to find out a week after Wales had won the Grand Slam when the newspaper carried a letter from a reader in Pontypridd:

> New rugby coach Warren Gatland has taken Wales to the Grand Slam. Wales boiled over at the recent game against France in Cardiff, and the Kiwi can't walk down the street without people slapping him on the back. He took over last December after we were beaten by Fiji in the World Cup. Since then we've defeated England, Scotland and Ireland. Quite a change from the eras of former Wales coaches Graham Henry and Steve Hansen. Whatever happened to those two deadbeats?

APPENDIX 1

....

MATCH ANALYSIS

THE RBS 6 NATIONS - TWICKENHAM - 02.02.08

ENGLAND			WALES	
15	Balshaw		1	Sheridan
14	Sackey		2	Regan
13	Tindall		3	**Vickery**
12	Flood		4	Shaw
11	Strettle		5	Borthwick
10	Wilkinson		6	Haskell
9	Gomarsall		7	Moody
			8	Narraway

ENGLAND 19 — WALES 26

16 HT 6

WALES				
15	Byrne		1	D J Jones
14	M A Jones		2	Bennett
13	Parker		3	A R Jones
12	Henson		4	Gough
11	S M Williams		5	A W Jones
10	Hook		6	J Thomas
9	Phillips		7	M E Williams
			8	**R P Jones**

England

Try	1
PenTry	0
Conversions	1 / 1
Penalty Goals	3 / 4
Drop Goals	1 / 1

Phases of Play

Scrums Won	4
Lost	0
Lineouts Won	10
Lost	0
Pens Conceded	7
Freekick Conceded	2
Mauls Won	1
Ruck and Drive	29
Ruck and Pass	47

Ball Won

In Open Play	77
In Opponent's 22	15
At Set Pieces	21
Turnovers Won	10

Team Statistics

Passes Completed	97
Line Breaks	5
Possession Kicked	32
Errors from Kicks	6
Kicks to Touch	9
Kicks / Passes	24%
Tackles Made	86
Missed	5
Tackle Completion	94%
Offloads in Tackle	8
Offloads / Tackled	9%
Total Errors Made	17
Errors / Ball Won	17%

Minutes in Possession

1	14:32	2	10:08

Mins in Opponent's Half

1	27:26	2	11:50

Match events

England	Time	Wales
WILKINSON - Penalty	1:06	
	3:23	HOOK - Penalty
WILKINSON - Penalty	10:30	
Vainikolo on for Strettle	13:56	
	14:13	Popham on for J Thomas
Rees on for Moody	15:31	
WILKINSON - Drop Goal	18:22	
FLOOD - Try	24:17	
WILKINSON - Conversion	25:23	
	38:28	HOOK - Penalty
WILKINSON - PenMiss	40:44	
	HT	
Kay on for Rees	0:05	
WILKINSON - Penalty	5:25	
	5:55	Jenkins on for A R Jones
	5:57	Shanklin on for Parker
	18:23	HOOK - Penalty
Mears on for Regan	18:44	
	18:47	Rees on for Bennett
	24:01	HOOK - Penalty
Cipriani on for Tindall	24:37	
	28:50	BYRNE - Try
	30:26	HOOK - Conversion
Stevens on for Vickery	30:41	
	31:18	PHILLIPS - Try
	33:23	HOOK - Conversion
	42:37	Evans on for A W Jones

Wales

Try	2
PenTry	0
Conversions	2 / 2
Penalty Goals	4 / 4
Drop Goals	0 / 0

Phases of Play

Scrums Won	11
Lost	0
Lineouts Won	10
Lost	4
Pens Conceded	7
Freekick Conceded	0
Mauls Won	1
Ruck and Drive	23
Ruck and Pass	43

Ball Won

In Open Play	67
In Opponent's 22	34
At Set Pieces	28
Turnovers Won	2

Team Statistics

Passes Completed	87
Line Breaks	4
Possession Kicked	26
Errors from Kicks	1
Kicks to Touch	6
Kicks / Passes	23%
Tackles Made	86
Missed	5
Tackle Completion	94%
Offloads in Tackle	4
Offloads / Tackled	4%
Total Errors Made	5
Errors / Ball Won	5%

Minutes in Possession

1	07:58	2	13:35

Mins in Opponent's Half

1	14:19	2	31:21

Top Carries

S M Williams	9
Sheridan	8
Byrne	7
Haskell	7
Henson	7

Top Tacklers

R P Jones	19
M E Williams	18
Narraway	16
Haskell	12
Popham	9

Most Missed Tackles

Haskell	2
Balshaw	1
Bennett	1
Henson	1
M E Williams	1

Most Off-Loads

Narraway	2
S M Williams	2
Shaw	2
Vainikolo	2
Byrne	1

Most Errors

Balshaw	4
Wilkinson	3
Gomarsall	2
Narraway	2
Tindall	2

SOFTWARE

Official data and competitive intelligence
partner of the RBS 6 Nations Championship

THE RBS 6 NATIONS - MILLENNIUM STADIUM - 09.02.08

	WALES			SCOTLAND	
15	Byrne	1	D J Jones	15	Southwell	1	Jacobsen
14	Roberts	2	Bennett	14	Walker	2	Ford
13	Shanklin	3	A R Jones	13	de Luca	3	Murray
12	Henson	4	Gough	12	Henderson	4	Hines
11	S M Williams	5	Evans	11	Paterson	5	Hamilton
10	Hook	6	J Thomas	10	Parks	6	**White**
9	Phillips	7	M E Williams	9	Blair	7	Barclay
		8	**R P Jones**			8	Brown

WALES 30 — SCOTLAND 15

10 HT 6

WALES				Timeline	SCOTLAND			
Try	3	PenTry	0		Try	0	PenTry	0
Conversions		3 / 3		10:14	Conversions		0 / 0	
Penalty Goals		3 / 3		13:05 — PATERSON - Penalty	Penalty Goals		5 / 5	
Drop Goals		0 / 0		S M WILLIAMS - Try — 13:05	Drop Goals		0 / 0	

Phases of Play				Phases of Play	
Scrums Won	7		HOOK - Conversion — 14:22	Scrums Won	6
Lost	0		14:22 / 17:14 *HINES - Sin Bin*	Lost	0
Lineouts Won	13		HOOK - Penalty — 17:14	Lineouts Won	15
Lost	2		32:40	Lost	2
Pens Conceded	10		36:08 — PATERSON - Penalty	Pens Conceded	6
Freekick Conceded	1		33:01 Hogg on for White	Freekick Conceded	0
Mauls Won	1		HT	Mauls Won	6
Ruck and Drive	48		42:20 Thomson on for Ford	Ruck and Drive	55
Ruck and Pass	39		HOOK - Try — 3:32 — PATERSON - Penalty	Ruck and Pass	8

Ball Won				Ball Won	
			HOOK - Conversion — 5:46		
In Open Play	88		7:16	In Open Play	69
In Opponent's 22	26		11:06 — PATERSON - Penalty	In Opponent's 22	15
At Set Pieces	26		Jenkins on for D J Jones — 13:20	At Set Pieces	31
Turnovers Won	6		16:29 — PATERSON - Penalty	Turnovers Won	2

Team Statistics				Team Statistics	
			S M Jones on for Hook — 18:44		
			Peel on for Phillips — 18:46		
Passes Completed	131		Rees on for Bennett — 18:49	Passes Completed	41
Line Breaks	11		22:50 Macleod on for Hines	Line Breaks	0
Possession Kicked	16		Delve on for R P Jones — 23:03	Possession Kicked	14
Errors from Kicks	4		S M JONES - Penalty — 25:50	Errors from Kicks	5
Kicks to Touch	8		S M WILLIAMS - Try — 28:23	Kicks to Touch	12
Kicks / Passes	10%		S M JONES - Conversion — 30:50	Kicks / Passes	25%
			31:50 Danielli on for Parks		
Tackles Made	87		31:59 Kerr on for Murray	Tackles Made	105
Missed	4		S M JONES - Penalty — 36:00	Missed	11
Tackle Completion	95%		Parker on for Shanklin — 36:28	Tackle Completion	90%
			37:56 Morrison on for De Luca		
Offloads in Tackle	12		D L Jones on for Gough — 38:00	Offloads in Tackle	6
Offloads / Tackled	11%		42:40 Cusiter on for Blair	Offloads / Tackled	6%
Total Errors Made	17			Total Errors Made	17
Errors / Ball Won	14%			Errors / Ball Won	17%

Minutes in Possession				Minutes in Possession			
1	14:10	2	14:22	1	13:13	2	14:31

Mins in Opponent's Half				Mins in Opponent's Half			
1	30:12	2	29:59	1	14:01	2	15:02

Top Carries		Top Tacklers		Most Missed Tackles		Most Off-Loads		Most Errors	
Brown	10	Barclay	14	Blair	3	Hook	3	R P Jones	4
R P Jones	10	A R Jones	13	Murray	2	Brown	2	Blair	3
M E Williams	8	Hamilton	12	Parks	2	Byrne	2	Paterson	3
Shanklin	8	M E Williams	12	Barclay	1	Hines	2	Southwell	3
J Thomas	7	Parks	12	Bennett	1	A R Jones	1	de Luca	2

Match Facts are supplied by SAS Software Ltd and recorded under the guidance and direction of
STEPHEN P SMITH (WRU REFEREE)
who objectively reports on ALL decisions made by the Match Officials

THE RBS 6 NATIONS - MILLENNIUM STADIUM - 23.02.08

	WALES				ITALY	
15	Byrne	1	Jenkins	15	Marcato	1	Perugini
14	M A Jones	2	Rees	14	Sgarbi	2	Ghiraldini
13	Shanklin	3	R Thomas	13	Canale	3	Castrogiovanni
12	Henson	4	Gough	12	M Bergamasco	4	Dellape
11	S M Williams	5	Evans	11	Galon	5	del Fava
10	S M Jones	6	J Thomas	10	Masi	6	Sole
9	Peel	7	M E Williams	9	Picone	7	M Bergamasco
		8	**R P Jones**			8	**Parisse**

WALES 47 — ITALY 8

HT 13 — 8

Try	5	PenTry	0		
Conversions	5 / 5				
Penalty Goals	4 / 4				
Drop Goals	0 / 0				

Italy			
Try	1	PenTry	0
Conversions	0 / 1		
Penalty Goals	1 / 2		
Drop Goals	0 / 1		

Match timeline

Wales	Time	Italy
S M JONES - Penalty	5:03	
S M JONES - Penalty	11:11	
	12:54	CASTROGIOVANNI - Try
	14:29	MARCATO - ConMiss
	21:30	Lo Cicero on for Castrogiovanni
BYRNE - Try	31:11	
S M JONES - Conversion	32:19	
	32:58	Castrogiovanni on for Lo Cicero
	35:00	MARCATO - PenMiss
	47:31	MARCATO - Penalty
	HT	
SHANKLIN - Try	1:52	
S M JONES - Conversion	2:39	
Phillips on for Peel	3:16	
	3:46	MARCATO - DropMiss
S M JONES - Penalty	7:34	
	10:07	*MI BERGAMASCO - Sin Bin*
S M JONES - Penalty	10:30	
	10:59	Lo Cicero on for Perugini
	11:03	Bortolami on for Dellape
	15:11	Buso on for Masi
Bennett on for Rees	17:36	
S M WILLIAMS - Try	19:42	
S M JONES - Conversion	20:43	
	21:16	Travagli on for Picone
	23:39	Zanni on for Sole
Hook on for S M Jones	31:03	
D J Jones on for R Thomas	31:12	
D L Jones on for Evans	31:20	
BYRNE - Try	31:51	
HOOK - Conversion	32:58	
Delve on for M E Williams	33:20	
	33:29	Festuccia on for Ghiraldini
Parker on for Henson	34:22	
	35:11	Perugini on for Castrogiovanni
S M WILLIAMS - Try	38:21	
HOOK - Conversion	39:21	

Phases of Play

Wales		Italy	
Scrums Won	6	Scrums Won	6
Lost	0	Lost	1
Lineouts Won	15	Lineouts Won	7
Lost	4	Lost	1
Pens Conceded	8	Pens Conceded	10
Freekick Conceded	1	Freekick Conceded	1
Mauls Won	3	Mauls Won	1
Ruck and Drive	58	Ruck and Drive	22
Ruck and Pass	47	Ruck and Pass	24

Ball Won

Wales		Italy	
In Open Play	108	In Open Play	47
In Opponent's 22	14	In Opponent's 22	14
At Set Pieces	31	At Set Pieces	21
Turnovers Won	4	Turnovers Won	6

Team Statistics

Wales		Italy	
Passes Completed	140	Passes Completed	71
Line Breaks	12	Line Breaks	4
Possession Kicked	30	Possession Kicked	31
Errors from Kicks	10	Errors from Kicks	7
Kicks to Touch	1	Kicks to Touch	9
Kicks / Passes	17%	Kicks / Passes	30%
Tackles Made	56	Tackles Made	135
Missed	3	Missed	20
Tackle Completion	94%	Tackle Completion	87%
Offloads in Tackle	19	Offloads in Tackle	5
Offloads / Tackled	14%	Offloads / Tackled	8%
Total Errors Made	24	Total Errors Made	17
Errors / Ball Won	17%	Errors / Ball Won	25%

Minutes in Possession

Wales				Italy			
1	13:46	2	18:00	1	12:23	2	09:35

Mins in Opponent's Half

Wales				Italy			
1	26:43	2	23:32	1	15:46	2	21:40

Top Carries

R P Jones	13
J Thomas	10
Byrne	9
M A Jones	9
Marcato	7

Top Tacklers

M Bergamasco	14
del Fava	13
Parisse	13
Dellape	12
Masi	10

Most Missed Tackles

Canale	3
del Fava	3
M Bergamasco	2
M E Williams	2
Masi	2

Most Off-Loads

Peel	5
Phillips	5
Marcato	3
S M Williams	3
M E Williams	2

Most Errors

Marcato	5
Byrne	4
S M Jones	4
Galon	3
Henson	3

Match Facts are supplied by SAS Software Ltd and recorded under the guidance and direction of
STEPHEN P SMITH (WRU REFEREE)
who objectively reports on ALL decisions made by the Match Officials

SAS SOFTWARE

Official data and competitive intelligence
partner of the RBS 6 Nations Championship

THE RBS 6 NATIONS - CROKE PARK - 08.03.08

	IRELAND				WALES	
15	Kearney	1	Horan	15	Byrne	1	Jenkins
14	Horgan	2	R Best	14	M A Jones	2	Rees
13	**BG O'Driscoll**	3	Hayes	13	Shanklin	3	A R Jones
12	Trimble	4	O'Callaghan	12	Henson	4	Gough
11	Bowe	5	O'Connell	11	S M Williams	5	A W Jones
10	O'Gara	6	Leamy	10	S M Jones	6	J Thomas
9	Reddan	7	D P Wallace	9	Phillips	7	M E Williams
		8	Heaslip			8	**R P Jones**

IRELAND 12 — WALES 16

6 | HT | 3

Ireland		Time	Event	Wales	
Try	0	PenTry	0		4:35	O'GARA - Penalty	Try	1	PenTry	0
Conversions	0 / 0		10:23		S M JONES - PenMiss	Conversions	1 / 1
Penalty Goals	4 / 4	O'GARA - Penalty	19:18		Penalty Goals	3 / 5
Drop Goals	0 / 0		28:38	S M JONES - Penalty	Drop Goals	0 / 0
		32:24	S M JONES - PenMiss		
		44:37	*PHILLIPS - Sin Bin*		

		HT			
		6:46	S M JONES - Penalty		
		12:38	S M WILLIAMS - Try		
		13:58	S M JONES - Conversion		
		23:17	*M E WILLIAMS - Sin Bin*		
	24:05	O'GARA - Penalty		
	26:46	Hook on for S M Jones		
O'GARA - Penalty	30:15		
Jackman on for Horan	34:16		
Buckley on for Hayes	34:22		
Fitzgerald on for B G O'driscoll	34:30		
	36:20	D J Jones on for A R Jones	
	41:18	Delve on for R P Jones	
	41:53	HOOK - Penalty	

Phases of Play

Ireland		Wales	
Scrums Won	6	Scrums Won	7
Lost	0	Lost	0
Lineouts Won	8	Lineouts Won	14
Lost	0	Lost	1
Pens Conceded	7	Pens Conceded	10
Freekick Conceded	3	Freekick Conceded	1
Mauls Won	4	Mauls Won	1
Ruck and Drive	35	Ruck and Drive	38
Ruck and Pass	41	Ruck and Pass	77

Ball Won

Ireland		Wales	
In Open Play	80	In Open Play	116
In Opponent's 22	6	In Opponent's 22	31
At Set Pieces	24	At Set Pieces	28
Turnovers Won	3	Turnovers Won	2

Team Statistics

Ireland		Wales	
Passes Completed	75	Passes Completed	147
Line Breaks	3	Line Breaks	7
Possession Kicked	33	Possession Kicked	28
Errors from Kicks	3	Errors from Kicks	1
Kicks to Touch	6	Kicks to Touch	2
Kicks / Passes	30%	Kicks / Passes	16%
Tackles Made	128	Tackles Made	89
Missed	10	Missed	7
Tackle Completion	92%	Tackle Completion	92%
Offloads in Tackle	7	Offloads in Tackle	6
Offloads / Tackled	7%	Offloads / Tackled	4%
Total Errors Made	10	Total Errors Made	8
Errors / Ball Won	9%	Errors / Ball Won	5%

Minutes in Possession

Ireland				Wales			
1	17:14	2	12:43	1	15:17	2	22:30

Mins in Opponent's Half

Ireland				Wales			
1	17:13	2	13:43	1	28:00	2	32:54

Top Carries
R P Jones	12
Kearney	10
A W Jones	9
J Thomas	9
Shanklin	9

Top Tacklers
J Thomas	12
O'Connell	12
Horan	11
O'Callaghan	11
Heaslip	9

Most Missed Tackles
Henson	3
Jenkins	2
Trimble	2
A R Jones	1
Byrne	1

Most Off-Loads
Byrne	2
Reddan	2
Shanklin	2
Phillips	1
S M Williams	1

Most Errors
O'Gara	2
S M Jones	2
S M Williams	2
Horgan	1
M E Williams	1

Match Facts are supplied by SAS Software Ltd and recorded under the guidance and direction of
FRED HOWARD
who objectively reports on ALL decisions made by the Match Officials

THE RBS 6 NATIONS - MILLENNIUM STADIUM - 15.03.08

	WALES			FRANCE	
15	Byrne	1	Jenkins		
14	M A Jones	2	Bennett		
13	Shanklin	3	A R Jones		
12	Henson	4	Gough		
11	S M Williams	5	A W Jones		
10	Hook	6	Thomas		
9	Phillips	7	M E Williams		
		8	**R P Jones**		

15	Floch	1	Barcella
14	Clerc	2	Szarzewski
13	Jauzion	3	Mas
12	Traille	4	**Nallet**
11	Malzieu	5	Thion
10	Skrela	6	Dusautoir
9	Elissalde	7	Ouedraogo
		8	Bonnaire

WALES 29 — FRANCE 12

9 HT 6

WALES				FRANCE	
Try	2	PenTry	0		
Conversions	2 / 2				
Penalty Goals	5 / 7				
Drop Goals	0 / 1				

Match Timeline

Wales	Time	France
BYRNE - DropMiss	1:59	
HOOK - Penalty	7:58	
HOOK - PenMiss	14:40	
HOOK - Penalty	18:42	
	20:17	ELISSALDE - Penalty
HOOK - Penalty	22:17	
HENSON - Sin Bin	44:04	
	44:58	ELISSALDE - Penalty
	HT	
HOOK - PenMiss	3:53	
	4:19	Servat on for Szarzewski
	7:53	ELISSALDE - Penalty
D J Jones on for Jenkins	9:20	
Jenkins on for D J Jones	13:38	
S M Jones on for Hook	16:42	
Rees on for Bennett	16:49	
S M WILLIAMS - Try	21:35	
S M JONES - Conversion	22:50	
	24:05	Vermeulen on for Ouedraogo
	24:09	Poux on for Mas
	26:10	Yachvili on for Elissalde
	26:16	Trinh-duc on for Skrela
S M JONES - Penalty	27:18	
	30:28	Heymans on for Floch
	34:57	YACHVILI - Penalty
Evans on for Gough	35:15	
D J Jones on for A R Jones	35:18	
S M JONES - Penalty	38:10	
	40:18	Mela on for Thion
M E WILLIAMS - Try	41:58	
S M JONES - Conversion	42:49	

FRANCE			
Try	0	PenTry	0
Conversions	0 / 0		
Penalty Goals	4 / 4		
Drop Goals	0 / 0		

Phases of Play

Wales		France	
Scrums Won	7	Scrums Won	3
Lost	0	Lost	1
Lineouts Won	11	Lineouts Won	9
Lost	2	Lost	2
Pens Conceded	8	Pens Conceded	7
Freekick Conceded	2	Freekick Conceded	0
Mauls Won	0	Mauls Won	5
Ruck and Drive	38	Ruck and Drive	54
Ruck and Pass	36	Ruck and Pass	51

Ball Won

Wales		France	
In Open Play	74	In Open Play	110
In Opponent's 22	14	In Opponent's 22	6
At Set Pieces	25	At Set Pieces	20
Turnovers Won	4	Turnovers Won	2

Team Statistics

Wales		France	
Passes Completed	81	Passes Completed	151
Line Breaks	4	Line Breaks	1
Possession Kicked	43	Possession Kicked	34
Errors from Kicks	4	Errors from Kicks	6
Kicks to Touch	8	Kicks to Touch	10
Kicks / Passes	34%	Kicks / Passes	18%
Tackles Made	128	Tackles Made	79
Missed	6	Missed	5
Tackle Completion	95%	Tackle Completion	94%
Offloads in Tackle	5	Offloads in Tackle	17
Offloads / Tackled	6%	Offloads / Tackled	13%
Total Errors Made	14	Total Errors Made	15
Errors / Ball Won	14%	Errors / Ball Won	11%

Minutes in Possession

Wales				France			
1	08:44	2	13:46	1	19:03	2	14:27

Mins in Opponent's Half

Wales				France			
1	22:57	2	25:09	1	19:14	2	19:00

Top Carries

R P Jones	10
Jauzion	8
Bonnaire	7
Henson	7
Phillips	7

Top Tacklers

R P Jones	20
M E Williams	13
Shanklin	12
A R Jones	10
Bonnaire	10

Most Missed Tackles

Bonnaire	1
Dusautoir	1
Henson	1
Hook	1
Jenkins	1

Most Off-Loads

Floch	3
Clerc	2
Elissalde	2
Skrela	2
Bonnaire	1

Most Errors

Jauzion	4
Skrela	4
Floch	3
Henson	3
Byrne	2

APPENDIX 2

···

2008 RBS SIX NATIONS REVIEW BY THE INTERNATIONAL RUGBY BOARD

THE 2006 RBS SIX NATIONS WAS THE FIRST tournament to be played since the 2007 Rugby World Cup. Therefore, the performances of the teams following that competition were always going to be of interest. Of the six participating teams, ENGLAND were the only one that came into the competition with a positive World Cup behind them. They had reached the final, whereas the other five teams had faltered on the way. Despite this, try scoring had proved difficult. In England's four matches against tier one countries (South Africa twice, Australia and France) they managed to score just one try. Therefore, it was interesting to see if England's Rugby World Cup success had created a level of confidence that would enable them to convert possession into points more effectively than in the past.

This was not to be. England scored just eight tries in five matches, which continued their declining try count over the years since 2001 – the records show that England's try count has dropped every single year since.

This declining try count happened in spite of England routinely obtaining more possession than any other team in the championship. This, however, changed in 2008. England obtained less possession than any other team, which explains why, quite exceptionally, England made fewer passes and created fewer rucks than any other side. Nevertheless, their defence remained strong – they conceded only four tries in five matches, which was less than half those conceded in 2007 – and despite the English forwards making proportionately more passes than ever before (and more than any other team), each one of England's tries were scored by their backs, two thirds of which came from set-piece possession.

When WALES won the Grand Slam in 2005, they showed a number of characteristics that were different from other teams. A number of those characteristics also applied in 2008:

- they put the ball into touch noticeably less than any other team;

- they kicked long at almost every restart – 25 out of 27;

- they scored more tries from opponents' handling errors and opponents' kicks than several of their opponents put together;

- they scored more tries from inside their own half than England, Scotland, Ireland and Italy combined.

There were, on the other hand, a number of substantial differences. Their forwards made proportionately fewer passes in 2008 than in 2005 (22 per cent of all passes down to 17 per cent). The major difference, however, was in defence. From conceding twenty-four tries in 2007 and 2006, they conceded just two in the 2008 campaign – the lowest figure ever achieved in the Six Nations Championship. Wales were a team, therefore, that managed to ally a huge defensive achievement with an ability to score tries from broken play and from play starting inside their own half, a common characteristic of successful teams. Twelve of their thirteen tries were scored by backs, their only forward try coming in the last five minutes of the final game. This try-scoring success was then supplemented by a high success rate of kicks at goal. A 100 per cent conversion success rate made every try worth seven points.

Another area showed noticeable change. From being the team that obtained the least overall possession in 2007, they became the second highest in 2008 with an increase of almost 35 per cent. Such increased possession contributed towards Wales becoming the team with the highest rate of rucking.

Another characteristic of Wales in 2008 was the greater intensity of performance in the second half of their matches. They did not concede a try in the second half – and 11 of their 13 tries were scored in that period. In addition, they were the only team to kick most of their penalty goals in the second half.

IRELAND saw a considerable change in fortune in 2008 compared with 2007. In 2008, they were the most successful team in turning possession into points – and were also the most efficient in preventing their opponents from scoring tries. This changed in 2008. While seventeen tries and fifteen tries were scored in the previous two tournaments, in 2008 Ireland managed just nine. Allied to this was the fact that the ten tries they conceded were twice as many as they conceded in 2007. Furthermore, they were the only team in the 2008 championship whose opponents required less time to score tries than last year, and the only team to concede at least one try in the second half of every game.

Another characteristic of the Ireland team in 2006 and 2007 was their high rate of passing. In 2007, for example, they passed at a higher rate than any other team, and with a consistently high completion rate. The fewest passes they made in a game in 2007 was 118 – in 2008, however, they made just eighty-two and eighty-four in two matches, the lowest figures in the tournament.

While Ireland's passing game fell back somewhat, one area that saw little change was the role of their forwards. Ireland's approach sees forwards as providers of the ball with backs as distributors. This resulted in 2008 in the Ireland forwards making a total of 66 passes in the entire tournament, or just over a half of those made by Wales's forwards. This proportion of passes made by their forwards at 11 per cent of the Irish total is now less than one half of the percentage seen by many other teams.

Historically, ITALY have consistently conceded a considerable number of tries – 22 in 2005 and 18 in 2007, for example. One of their priorities in 2008, therefore, was to reduce the number of tries conceded to a more competitive level in the hope that they could equal, if not improve on, their performance in the 2007 Six Nations when they had two victories. Some of this was achieved. Although only one win was recorded, five fewer tries were conceded, bringing the 2007 total down from eighteen to thirteen – but they and Ireland were the only teams to concede at least one try in every game.

Conversely, however, they and Wales were the only teams to score a try in all five matches. Five of the six Italian tries did not contain a single pass, coming largely from scrums, lineouts and mauls and being scored by forwards.

In terms of the constituent elements of the game, Italy performed well. They obtained more possession than their opponents in three of their five games, they topped the lineout possession figures and had the highest scrum success rate of all five teams. What is also noticeable is that Italy forwards are now more liable to pass the ball than in the past, with their back row being the most likely of all teams' back rows to distribute the ball.

SCOTLAND won just one game in the 2007 Six Nations. They were the least effective team in turning possession into points, as well as being one of the least effective teams in preventing their opponents from scoring tries. Little changed in the 2008 Six Nations. In 2007, they scored seven tries. In 2008, they managed to score just three tries in one hundred minutes of possession, thereby requiring some thirty-three minutes of possession to score a try. All three came from set-piece possession – none from broken play. The result was that of all Scotland's points, just 22 per cent were accounted for by tries. The paucity of tries is also unfortunate in view of Scotland's outstanding place kicking record. All three tries were converted, and fifteen of sixteen penalty attempts were successful.

Conceding tries also continued to be a problem. Together with Italy, the 13 tries conceded by Scotland were the most in the tournament. Scottish forwards, especially their second row, invariably produce a relatively high proportion of passes, and this year was no exception. Their second row passed the ball on almost one in two occasions – an extremely high proportion compared with most other teams. Scotland were also the most effective in obtaining opposition ball at the lineout. Despite this, try scoring remained a major problem.

FRANCE had a new coach in 2008. What was of potential interest was to see what their approach would be, since evidence suggests that France have two distinct and contrasting ways of playing. There is the relatively conservative approach of recent years, where kicking has been more noticeable than passing, an approach that contrasted dramatically with the game plan adopted by France in the match against Scotland in 2007. This involved a constant recycling of the ball, which produced an approach that was seen by some as being more typically French.

Certainly, an element of this latter approach appeared at times throughout the tournament:

- ten of their eleven tries were scored by backs;
- five tries were scored from turnovers out of a; tournament total of eleven
- over half of their tries were scored from inside their own half.

Such scores, however, did not come from the sort of expansive game that involves all 15 players handling the ball. While France were the team that passed the most, and their rate of passes successfully completed was the highest – albeit marginally – the French forwards made only 12 per cent of all passes, which is a low figure compared with several other countries whose percentage was nearer twice this figure. It would be premature, however, to draw too many conclusions from this year's tournament. Well over thirty players were chosen for the five matches as options were evaluated. Things will become somewhat clearer in next year's tournament.

Finally, the tournament itself produced some data of interest:

- average ball in play exceeded 50 per cent for the first time;

- one game (Wales v. France) reached 57 per cent, or forty-six minutes and eight seconds, the highest ever recorded;

- this increase largely came about because of a reduction in lineouts from 31 to 28 and a reduction in the number of scores;

- there was a noticeable reduction in tries but an increase in the number of penalty goals;

- more tries came from broken play and fewer from set-piece possession;

- of the thirty tries scored by the top three teams – Wales, England and France – twenty-eight were scored by the backs.